TABLE OF CONTENTS

Top 20 Test Taking Tips

1. Carefully follow all the test registration procedures
2. Know the test directions, duration, topics, question types, how many questions
3. Setup a flexible study schedule at least 3-4 weeks before test day
4. Study during the time of day you are most alert, relaxed, and stress free
5. Maximize your learning style; visual learner use visual study aids, auditory learner use auditory study aids
6. Focus on your weakest knowledge base
7. Find a study partner to review with and help clarify questions
8. Practice, practice, practice
9. Get a good night's sleep; don't try to cram the night before the test
10. Eat a well balanced meal
11. Know the exact physical location of the testing site; drive the route to the site prior to test day
12. Bring a set of ear plugs; the testing center could be noisy
13. Wear comfortable, loose fitting, layered clothing to the testing center; prepare for it to be either cold or hot during the test
14. Bring at least 2 current forms of ID to the testing center
15. Arrive to the test early; be prepared to wait and be patient
16. Eliminate the obviously wrong answer choices, then guess the first remaining choice
17. Pace yourself; don't rush, but keep working and move on if you get stuck
18. Maintain a positive attitude even if the test is going poorly
19. Keep your first answer unless you are positive it is wrong
20. Check your work, don't make a careless mistake

Reading and Language Arts

Language arts study

Anything having to do with communication, whether written or verbal, is included under the umbrella of language arts. In actual practice, most schools focus on the written aspects, including:
- Reading
- Writing
- Spelling
- Vocabulary
- Reading comprehension
- Literature

Other elements of a comprehensive language arts curriculum include:
- Speech
- Listening
- Verbal expression
- Listening comprehension

These various elements are often also included in other areas of the curriculum (such as social studies, history, and science) where reading, comprehension skills, specialized vocabulary, and proper spelling of subject-specific terms are important to the learning experience. Literature is also often incorporated into other areas, since both non-fiction and fiction literature can increase student engagement and place historical events into context.

Emergent literacy

Emergent literacy is a concept developed by Mary M. Clay in 1966. It refers to a stage in educational development when children begin to formally learn how to read and write. During this process, students begin to understand the printed word and how it relates to spoken language.

The use of the term has changed over the years. In current usage, it refers to the development of behavior related to literacy, or simply to the developmental phase when children begin to understand printed language. This phase covers childhood development from birth to approximately five years old.

Different definitions and concepts exist in regard to emergent literacy. Some educators feel that emergent literacy should be seen as a transitional period rather than as a specific stage as suggested by Clay (1966). During this transitional stage, a student gradually shifts from a nonreader to an emergent, or beginning, reader. The exact age at which this occurs varies from one child to another.

With a teacher taking on the role of getting a child ready to read, transmission educators feel that that readiness can be taught. Other theories posit that children must exhibit certain signs of readiness before any reading instruction will be effective.

Developmentally appropriate materials, curriculum and classrooms

Materials used to teach reading must be developmentally appropriate to the students being taught. Developmental appropriateness typically involves two major elements:

- Age appropriateness - Curriculum and materials should not be too advanced or too simplistic for the age of the student or students being taught. Materials are more likely to facilitate learning if they are relevant and engaging.
- Individual appropriateness - Materials should appeal to individual students, matching both individual ability and individual interest.

In general, materials that focus exclusively on skills often fail to engage students because they do not appeal to age-specific interests nor do they present reading as an entertaining activity. Curriculum that focuses solely on reading skills also tend to exclude writing, which is as important as reading in developing early literacy.

Determining a child's readiness to learn to read

Three major skills are often cited as indicating a child's entering the emergent literacy stage, and thus being ready to learn to read:

- Identifying the parts of a book - A child exhibiting reading readiness can differentiate between the title of a book, the book's beginning, end, and possibly chapter breaks.
- Understanding print directionality - In order to begin to learn to read, a child must understand the direction in which print is to be read (from left to right).
- Understanding the connection between spoken and printed language - A child exhibiting reading readiness understands that written or printed text is a graphical representation of the spoken word.

Reading readiness skills

Teachers or parents wishing to teach children to read can assess the signs of reading readiness. These concepts can also be taught if a child is old enough but has not yet completely absorbed these concepts.

- Parts of a book - The teacher can show the student the different parts of a book, then assess understanding by asking the student to tell her where the parts are and what they are called.

- Text directionality - Several teaching strategies can be used to teach directionality, such as marking the opposing sides of a book to indicate reading direction. Assessment is best achieved by observation.
- Connection between text and speech - Reading aloud to a child is an excellent way to present the concept that text is a representation of spoken words. Many children model this behavior by pretending to read aloud, indicating their comprehension of the concept.

Phonemes and graphemes

Understanding the connection between print and speech involves understanding the connection between phonemes and graphemes. Students do not need to be aware of these terms in order to understand the concept. The term phoneme refers to the actual sounds produced in a spoken word. Graphemes are the symbols, such as our alphabet, diacritical marks, or other parts of written language, that represent individual sounds of speech. When an adult reads aloud to a child while the child observes, the child often begins to recognize that certain combinations of symbols represent specific words. The ability to make these connections indicates reading readiness.

Define shared reading and reading aloud

If an adult reads aloud to a child, the child will make connections between text and speech more quickly. Children whose parents read aloud to them before they enter school or begin any formal reading instruction learn more quickly when formal instruction begins.

In shared reading, the adult typically reads aloud with the child following along, observing words as they are read. The child can participate in reading aloud when he or she sees a familiar word or words that are repeated throughout the text. Shared reading is effective for older students, as well, when materials are more difficult than those usually used for individual reading.

Neurological-impress method of shared reading

The neurological-impress method (NIM) was described in 1969 by R.G. Heckleman as a method in which adults and children hold the book together, with the adult reading aloud while the child observes and reads aloud when he recognizes words or repeated phrases. The adult can also point to the words and read them aloud together with the child. This approach helps the student not only to recognize words, but to learn correct pronunciation, phrasing and intonation. It also provides immediate feedback that builds the emergent reader's confidence and reinforces the connection between the spoken and written word. Perhaps most importantly, it provides a pleasant experience for the child.

Environmental print

Environmental print refers to the printed words we see every day. This can include traffic signs, words seen on television, newspapers, magazines, signs on buildings, and on the computer. Children can absorb the importance of this printed language through constant exposure and guidance by an adult. Since some of these signs are meant to provide information or to enforce rules and guidelines, children will find knowledge of the words' meanings to be important. Because the meanings of many of these words are so reliant on context, it will be easier for children to make the connections between environmental print and the importance of being able to read.

Language experience approach (LEA)

In the language experience approach, or LEA, to language development, children learn from experience rather than from traditional printed classroom materials such as leveled readers. An example of an LEA approach would be having the class write a report based on a group experience such as a field trip. The class writes this report together, reinforcing the ideas that:

- What the students say aloud can be rendered into print
- What is written down can be rendered back into speech
- Not only the student's own report, but also the reports of others can be written down and read back

LEA can be used to facilitate language acquisition and development, but is also used throughout school when groups of students work together to record a specific experience or activity.

Successful teaching strategy for language acquisition

In order to be successful, a teaching strategy for language acquisition must appeal to the students. Major characteristics that will increase the likelihood of meaningful engagement include:

- Authenticity - Materials should relate to students' real life experiences, making them more relevant.
- Books with meaningful stories - In addition to working with skills, materials should include actual books that tell a meaningful story.
- Not overly repetitive - Materials should not repeat themselves, but match the students' existing knowledge levels and provide some challenge.
- Appropriate - Teaching materials should be developmentally, individually and age appropriate for the student or students using them.

Teachers should be prepared to use different strategies for different students, as well as to provide additional, appropriate materials for those students who might be learning more slowly or more quickly than others in the class.

Invented spelling

Since individual sounds in English can be spelled in many different ways, children often use invented spelling when they begin to develop written language skills. These spellings are based on their limited understanding of what letters and combinations of letters make specific sounds, but do not always correspond to accepted spelling rules in English. Nor do they take into account the numerous variations in spellings and exceptions to spelling rules that are common in English. As the child reads more and is exposed to a wider variety of written language, he or she will absorb some of these rules on their own. Rules, exceptions and other elements of written language and spelling will also be part of the student's formal educational experience. Eventually, the student will move from invented spelling to standardized spelling.

Stages of literacy as presented by Martha Combs

In 1966, Marie M. Clay posited the idea of the emerging literacy stage in intellectual development. Forty years later, in 2006, Martha Combs proposed two additional stages in literacy development in children. The Combs model includes:
- Stage 1: Emerging literacy - Similar to Clay's concept of emerging literacy, this stage sees children in transition between spoken and written language with the help of adults.
- Stage 2: Developing literacy - In this stage, children begin to develop independent literacy skills, including decoding and handwriting. This stage typically occurs during the first and second grades.
- Stage 3: Transitional reading - Children need little help with their reading and can read and write independently while gradually developing higher-level skills and comprehension. This level typically refers to second grade and higher.

Spelling development as posited by J.R. Gentry

In 1981, J.R. Gentry defined five stages in the development of spelling skills:
1. Pre-communication – The child uses letters randomly without a clear idea of their meaning or use.
2. Pre-phonetic – The child begins to understand the use of letters and how they connect to sounds. During this stage, the child starts to use some letters correctly.
3. Phonetic - The child understands the concept of spelling and tends to spell words phonetically.
4. Transitional - The child begins to understand some basic spelling rules and spells some words correctly while still spelling other words phonetically.
5. Correct spelling - The child understands spelling rules and spells most words correctly.

Phonics

Phonics has been the most common strategy for teaching reading for literally hundreds of years. In 1839, the McGuffey Reader, developed by William Holmes McGuffy, became a popular textbook to teach reading. The reader taught not only phonics concepts but also moral concepts acceptable at the time. The reader was still widely used in 1920, when it sold 122 million copies.

Another important influence on the use of phonics in schools was Rudolf Flesch. His book, Why Johnny Can't Read—And What You Can Do About It, was published in 1955. The book suggested that the reduction of American literacy was due to schools no longer using phonics to teach reading, but shifting to other techniques that came into vogue in the 1920s and later.

Phonics has remained prominent in teaching reading for so many years because it presents numerous advantages over other methods.

Among these are:
- Provides children with tools they can use to decode words with which they are unfamiliar
- Works well for auditory learners because of its focus on the sounds of language
- Using phonics methods to learn to read often leads to better spelling skills

Because of these advantages, the International Reading Association (IRA) has stated that phonics is an important approach for teaching reading.

In order to ensure success in teaching phonics, language arts teachers should consider using some of the following techniques:
- Provide phonics instruction that is sequential, systematic and structured.
- Allow students to practice phonics rules in the context of everyday encounters with written language.
- Allow students to practice phonics skills in the context of meaningful materials such as books or magazines relevant to their interests.
- Do not teach phonics isolated from meaningful material, such as teaching phonics with lists of words rather than sentences and stories.

These techniques help students decode words using phonics techniques while at the same time encountering and learning exceptions to basic phonics rules. They also increase student engagement by providing materials that are meaningful and engaging to the students.

Phonics is based on the idea of the connection between phonemes and graphemes. Phonemes are the actual sounds created during speech; graphemes are the symbols, such as single letters or combinations of letters, that are used to represent these spoken sounds visually. Students are taught to "sound out" words based on what sounds correspond to the letters used to spell the word, and vice-versa with written language. During early stages of phonics learning, students use invented spellings. As learning progresses, students learn spelling rules, including exceptions and alternate spellings of certain sounds. The phonics approach gradually leads from spelling phonetically to spelling according to standard spelling rules.

Although phonics has long been presented as the most effective way to teach reading, it does present some disadvantages, including:
- Does not always work well for visual learners
- Spelling rules in English are not consistent, meaning that phonics rules do not always apply
- Children can be confused by the numerous exceptions inherent in phonics as it applies to the English language

Many of these disadvantages can be avoided by using phonics as a part of an overall literacy program that includes other approaches. In this way, children who do not learn as well with phonics can have the option of learning to read in a different way and children who do well with phonics will be exposed to other literacy concepts.

Phonemic awareness

Phonemic awareness occurs when an emergent reader begins to associate the sounds of spoken language with the symbols of written language. As children acquire spoken language skills, they learn how to pronounce the sounds of that language. In English, this consists of about 44 separate sounds. Phonemic awareness begins when the child starts to realize that individual sounds can be represented by letters or combinations of letters. In English acquisition, this means learning the ways in which the 26 letters of the alphabet are used singly and in combinations to represent these sounds.

Structural analysis

Structural analysis refers to the ability to analyze words according to their individual parts, or syllables. A reader who understands the concepts of word structure can more easily sound out unfamiliar words. Structural analysis benefits from knowledge of phonics rules, which can affect the way each syllable is pronounced based on the structure of the rest of the word. It is also helpful to understand concepts such as prefixes and suffixes, as this element of structural analysis can not only help the reader pronounce the word, but can also give clues to the meaning of the word.

Some of the basic rules that help guide structural analysis of words include:
- Pronunciation of specific word endings
- Rules regarding where words are divided into syllables
- Pronunciation of prefixes
- Meanings of prefixes and suffixes

For young readers, these rules are most useful when they encounter words that are similar to words they already know. For example, if a child already knows a basic word, then encounters the same word with a prefix or suffix, the child will recognize the root word and, if he or she knows the rules of structural analysis, will be able to pronounce it as well as ascertain its approximate meaning.

v/cv and the vc/cv rules

The v/cv and the vc/cv rules refer to how words are properly divided into syllables. In this case, v stands for vowel and c stands for consonant. In order to apply this rule a reader must know which letters are vowels and which are consonants. In the v/cv rule, the syllable division occurs between the first vowel and its following consonant. In the vc/cv rule, the division occurs between two adjacent consonants. For example, the word "afraid" is divided into syllables as "a-fraid," dividing between the leading vowel and its following consonant according to the v/cv rule. A word like "winter" follows the vc/cv rule, being divided as "win-ter." These rules can help readers break words down into syllables, making pronunciation easier.

Compound word rule

The compound word rule is when two words are joined together to form a single word; this word is known as a compound word. When the word is broken into syllables, a syllable break occurs between the two separate words. If a reader is familiar with both words that form the compound word, he or she will likely be able to determine how to divide the word into syllables in order to understand its proper pronunciation. In most cases, he or she will also be able to determine the definition of the word based on the meanings of the familiar words that make up the compound word.

Other approaches to teaching reading besides phonics

Other methods for teaching reading include:
- Sight word method - Children are taught to recognize words by sight rather than learning to decode them. A sight word approach to teaching reading can severely limit vocabulary and does not provide the student with decoding rules.
- Modified alphabet - Diacritical marks are added to the traditional alphabet to make the correspondence between specific letters and specific sounds more direct. Instruction gradually phases to the traditional alphabet.

- Whole language - Children are encouraged to learn from extensive exposure to various literature. It includes elements of both the phonics and sight word methods.

Controlled vocabulary

In a controlled vocabulary situation, emerging readers are only exposed to reading materials that contain certain words. New words are gradually introduced over time, giving the reader time to learn them. Many books aimed at beginning readers use controlled vocabulary to increase exposure to certain families of words. As the texts become more advanced, more varied vocabulary is used. In this way, readers gradually build their vocabulary and comprehension.

Context clues

When faced with an unfamiliar word, students must not only be able to decode its pronunciation, but also its meaning. Context clues are one of the most important tools in this kind of comprehension. By analyzing the familiar words around an unfamiliar word, or by analyzing specific parts of the unfamiliar word, students can often deduce the word's meaning. For example, a familiar suffix or prefix on a word can give an important clue to the word's meaning. The placement of a word in a sentence can tell the reader whether it is a noun, verb, adjective or other part of speech. The content of the remaining parts of the sentence can also provide clues as to the word's meaning.

Language cues used in decoding word pronunciation and meaning

The three major types of language cues are:
1. Syntactic - This refers to the order of words, how they are placed in a sentence and how they appear to function within that sentence. A reader can often deduce whether a word is a noun or a verb based upon its placement and function in a sentence. This can also include prefixes and suffixes that affect the meaning of a word.
2. Semantic - These are clues toward the meaning of a word derived from the full context of that word. Clues could come from the individual sentence where the word is placed or from a larger section of the text such as a paragraph or the entire text.
3. Phonemes and graphemes - These provide pronunciation clues. The phoneme is the spoken sound while the grapheme is the written symbol used to represent that sound.

Scaffolding

Scaffolding refers to the need for teachers to support readers of all levels in a classroom. In any group of children, different individuals will be at different learning levels and have different learning approaches. They would need different types of support, encouragement and even different learning materials to ensure the best possible results. Some children, for example, might be advanced enough to read entirely on their own, while others in the same classroom might need more individualized instruction. Typical elements of scaffolding include guiding, demonstrating, and teaching.

Scaffolding typically consists of five different stages that indicate the level of support provided by the teacher. These five stages are:

1. Modeled - The teacher models reading tasks for the student, who primarily observes but can also participate. Reading aloud would be a modeled reading task.
2. Shared - The teacher and the student read the text together. The student can read familiar words while the teacher models reading of unfamiliar words.
3. Interactive - The teacher and student continue to work together as the student takes on more of the reading.
4. Guided - The teacher works with the student to provide help where it is still needed, such as supplying pronunciations or meanings for unfamiliar words.
5. Independent - The student is able to read on his or her own.

Visualizing and inferences

As a reader absorbs a text, he or she visualizes the events, people and places described within it. This process of visualization helps increase the understanding of what they are reading as well as causing a higher level of engagement with the text.

If they understand the text, readers make inferences naturally as they read. Prior knowledge can be combined with textual clues to allow the reader to guess what might happen next or to garner additional information about occurrences or characters that is not explicitly presented in the text.

Activating prior knowledge and asking questions

Two important reading strategies for both comprehension and engagement are:

1. Activating prior knowledge - Texts that are relevant to the student will naturally engage the student more thoroughly. Using prior knowledge, a student can relate the current text to past experiences as well as their current understanding and issues beyond his or her individual situation, adding a more personal meaning to the text overall.
2. Asking questions - A reader who is engaged in a text will ask questions about what has happened and even about what will happen next. Predicting what is coming next in a text is an important part of comprehension and involves thorough engagement with and understanding of the text.

Determination of important ideas and information synthesis

A reader wishing to derive essential information from a text must be able to determine which ideas in the text are most important. This skill is illustrated when a student is studying for a test; he or she must be able to sort through large quantities of information to determine which concepts are the most important.

Information synthesis occurs when a reader assimilates new information, combining it with things he or she already knows. This kind of combination of information can lead to new ideas, understandings, theories or insights. Synthesizing information is essential for higher level learning and comprehension.

Repairing understanding and confirmation

If, as a student is reading, he or she experiences confusion over the text, they must take the time to backtrack and "repair" their understanding of the specific text. This can involve rereading the text, looking up unfamiliar words, or asking for assistance in understanding a specific passage.
Confirmation occurs as predictions made by the reader are either confirmed or contradicted. If a reader's prediction is confirmed by the text, the student can be rewarded by knowing he or she made a correct guess. If the prediction is contradicted, he or she can be rewarded by the surprise of an unexpected conclusion or development in the text.

Teaching reading strategies student/teacher interaction

Teachers can use a variety of approaches when teaching reading strategies. A structured approach includes:
- Modeling the strategy
- Explaining the strategy
- Describing how to apply the strategy
- Providing guided practice of the strategy

The teacher can narrate their thought processes while modeling the strategy while the students do the same while applying it. This can clarify how the strategy is used and help students understand it more clearly. As the strategy is practiced in the classroom, the teacher can provide feedback and assistance to ensure the strategy is effectively utilized.

Literal and interpretive levels of reading comprehension

In the literal level of reading comprehension, the reader understands the literal, straightforward meaning of the text. To determine if a student has understood the text on a literal level, the teacher can ask questions referring to:

- Facts in the text
- Details found in the text
- Sequence of events
- Comparing one detail of the text to another

In the interpretive level of reading comprehension, the reader begins to interpret various types of language and make inferences based on the text. Questions to determine interpretive comprehension could cover:

- Point of view of the text
- Definitions of terms
- Explanations of figurative language
- The author's basic message or purpose
- Requiring the reader to infer answers from the text

Parts of a book and reflecting

Books often provide different sections such as maps, indices, tables of contents, charts or other tools that can help increase understanding as the student is reading. For example, a description of the Battle of the Bulge might be difficult for a student to understand unless he consults a map included in the text.

Reflection occurs after reading is completed. The student reflects on what he or she has read, considering its meaning and what they understand in a larger context. Reflection in a journal can be a useful classroom tool to increase and evaluate comprehension.

Comprehension

Successful reading involves more than simply decoding words. Reading comprehension involves understanding what is being read. Elements of comprehension include:

- Point of view of the text
- Message of the text
- Purpose of the author
- Opinion vs. fact
- Identifying facts and details
- Making inferences
- Identifying and understanding the conclusion

In addition, there are four basic levels of comprehension:
1. Literal
2. Interpretive
3. Critical
4. Creative

The teacher's work in the classroom should focus on helping students develop these specific comprehension skills and progress through the levels of comprehension to develop higher level thinking skills.

In the critical level of comprehension, the student must make judgments based on the text. Elements the student might address include:
- Is the text reliable?
- What is the reader's emotional response to the text?
- How does the text compare to other texts?
- Is the text based on facts or on the author's opinions?
- Is the author an informed source?

The creative level is the highest level of comprehension. In this level of comprehension, the student has reached a level where he or she can use information from the text and apply it to other similar situations. The teacher could ask the students to:
- Come up with different solutions to a problem presented in the text
- Compose a different ending to a story
- Consider how the story might have progressed if a specific plot element were changed

Monitoring understanding

Teachers can help students use comprehension strategies and ensure they can monitor student progress in comprehension using a variety of techniques. These can include:
- Encouraging students to reread and/or read ahead to increase comprehension
- Have students discuss parts of the text that are unclear
- Teach students to use discussion, journaling techniques, or notation to keep track of their thought processes while they are reading
- Teach students to be aware when they lose focus and be prepared to backtrack if necessary
- Addressing all student questions
- Teach students to use different strategies depending upon what problems are encountered in the text

Convergent questions, divergent questions and cloze tests

Traditional questioning techniques can help assess reading comprehension in a testing environment or other type of assessment. Three major types of questioning are:
1. Convergent questions, which have only one correct answer.
2. Divergent questions, which have more than one correct answer.
3. Cloze tests, in which words are left out of a passage and the student must fill them in.

In cloze tests, different approaches can be used, such as requiring the student to fill the blank with the exact word. If the test focuses on meaning rather than recall, a synonym might be acceptable.

SQ3R

SQ3R is an acronym for a reading comprehension method whose steps are:
- Survey - Skim the text and look at major characteristics such as headings of chapters, diagrams, charts or pictures, and words that are emphasized by a different font.
- Question - Produce a list of questions the text might answer. A list of questions at the end of the text might be helpful in this step.
- Read - Read through the text to find answers to the chosen questions.
- Recite - Read through the questions and attempt to answer them without referring to the text.
- Review - Look over the text to see if the answers supplied are correct.

Graphic organizers

Graphic organizers can help provide a visible record of students' comprehension. Some types of graphic organizers include:
- Venn diagrams - These diagrams are made up of overlapping circles and demonstrate similarities and differences between specific ideas or objects.
- Fishbone organizers - These charts, so named because of their similarity to fish skeletons, display the connections between cause and effect.
- Double-entry journals - Students record quotes from the relevant text in these journals, along with their comments or analysis in an adjacent column.
- Thinking maps or webs - These diagrams are usually constructed with a main concept at the center and related concepts branching off and surrounding the main concept. Subordinate concepts can be connected via arrows and can lead to more extensive webs leading off the main web.

Reading speed

How fast a student reads can sometimes be relevant in assessing his or her comprehension level. Students who have difficulty with comprehension may read much more slowly or might spend extra time backtracking to reread sections, indicating difficulty with general comprehension. On the other hand, students who read very fast might not be taking the time to ensure complete understanding of details. Recording reading speeds and comparing the speed to the level of comprehension can help determine if an individual student's reading speed is related to lower comprehension scores.

PROVE

The PROVE method was proposed as an alternative to SQ3R. In the PROVE method, the reader develops his or her own strategy for evaluating a text rather than following the set strategy of SQ3R. PROVE consists of five steps:

1. Purpose - The student compiles questions to guide their reading, or determines the purpose of reading the text.
2. Read - The student reads the text.
3. Organize - The student sketches an outline displaying the major ideas in a text, with details added showing how they support the main ideas.
4. Vocabulary - The student makes note of new vocabulary or unfamiliar concepts.
5. Evaluate - The student looks over their notes as well as the text to see if they have achieved the purpose outlined in the first step.

Effective vocabulary instruction

Effective vocabulary instruction is important to nearly every subject, not just language arts. In order to effectively learn vocabulary in any subject, a student needs more than simply a list of words and their definitions. Major elements of vocabulary instruction include:
- Using new vocabulary in a meaningful context
- Repetition
- Relating vocabulary words to students' experience
- Encouraging students to read
- Providing students with opportunities to use new vocabulary

Some specific strategies for enforcing vocabulary instruction include:
- Word wall with new vocabulary posted regularly
- Lessons on decoding unfamiliar words
- Lessons about word classifications such as synonyms and antonyms
- Ways to study words

K-W-L charts and process guides

Pre-reading strategies can increase comprehension by helping students understand what to focus on while they are reading. One pre-reading strategy is the Know-Want-Learned, or K-W-L chart. Before reading, students make a list of what they already know about the text; then they list what they want to know about the subject or story. Finally, after reading the text, students can add what they learned to the chart.

Process guides include reading aids a teacher develops for a specific text or part of a text, for the entire class or individual students. They focus on problem areas the teacher has identified. Process guides can include terms, concepts, people or questions that students should watch for. Process guides take time to put together, but can often be reused.

Prose

The majority of educational texts used in teaching are written in prose. This includes textbooks, non-fiction, and fiction. Textbooks focused specifically on reading skills might also include sections of poetry.

Major types of prose include narrative, which can be either fiction or non-fiction and typically tells a story. The structure of the narrative can be linear or non-linear depending on the purpose of the author.

Literature is written material generally considered to be of particularly high quality or importance. Traditional literature tends to follow established patterns of storytelling. This term is usually used to mean literature that has been passed down for many years or even centuries. Modern literature can be more experimental and can also refer to works written more recently.

Poetry

Poetry can be particularly appealing to children because of its rhythmic nature. Children can make connections based on rhythm and rhyming sounds that they might not make with prose writings. Recognizing similar words and similar spellings by sight can also help early readers make connections between phonemes and graphemes. Even children who do not yet understand the spoken language can respond to the rhythms and sounds of poetry when it is read aloud. As children grow older, poetry continues to increase higher level comprehension skills by using metaphor, imagery, and other complex concepts.

Matching students with texts at appropriate reading levels

One common way to determine a student's reading level is through a cloze test. In a cloze test, words are left out of a representative text and the student must fill in the blanks. The student's reading level can be determined based on the score he or she receives on the cloze test; allowing the teacher to choose texts that match the student's abilities.

In addition, it is important to match texts to students' interests, especially if texts are to be used for reading practice or enrichment. Students will be more likely to read on their own if they can find texts that provide a sufficient challenge and appeal to their individual interests.

Book organization

Teachers can help students increase their reading comprehension by explaining the way a book is structured and the importance of different parts of the book. This can include the table of contents, the index, chapter headings, words that are presented in bold or italic text, or other divisions such as chapter subdivisions or sidebar text. These parts of a book will not be the same in every text, so the teacher should be prepared to discuss the structure of each individual text. When students are introduced to a book's structure before they begin to read it, they are less likely to be confused when encountering a non-traditional layout and will be better able to understand what they are reading without being distracted by different organization or different typefaces.

Guided practice and independent practice

In guided practice, the teacher watches students as they read to ensure they are using appropriate comprehension strategies, to help when necessary, and to assess the skill levels of individual students. The teacher can correct inaccurate pronunciation or interpretation and can supply definitions or other necessary information if the student requires assistance. Guided practice helps the teacher ensure that students understand the material.

In independent practice, students read on their own. The teacher can assess understanding after each reading session during a review or by having students report on what they have read.

Writing development

One accepted series of stages in the development of writing skills, outlined by Alexander Luria, is:
1. Undifferentiated stage - Consists of prewriting, when children from age three to age five begin to make random marks in imitation of adult writing.
2. Differentiated stage - At about age four, a child starts to understand that there is a relationship between marks on a page and spoken words. This is reflected in his use of more representative prewriting.

3. Pictographic stage - This stage occurs between ages four and six, and represents the child's understanding of the meaning of writing and what it is for.

Process writing

Process writing focuses on the stages a person takes when writing, with each stage leading to further refinement of the final written text. These stages are:
1. Prewriting - Students research and gather information on their chosen topic.
2. Writing - Students produce a rough first draft, without worrying about proper spelling, grammar or formatting.
3. Revising - Students review and revise their rough draft to improve mechanics.
4. Editing and evaluation - (Also called postwriting) Students evaluate their own work as well as that of other students.
5. Rewriting - Students revise their draft once again based on feedback from others during the editing and evaluation stage.
6. Publishing - Students "publish" the work by making and presenting a final, carefully written draft.

Standard American English

The formal or semi-formal language used in classrooms, on television, in written texts and textbooks is known as Standard American English. Though some creative writing reproduces individual dialects of English, narrative and informational texts are based on Standard American English. In a typical classroom, there are likely to be students who are more familiar with Standard syntax, grammar and vocabulary than others. In order to thoroughly understand educational materials and to effectively communicate in the classroom, all students need to learn Standard American English.

Language Experience Approach (LEA) and Standard American English

In Language Experience Approach (LEA), students discuss their experiences and the teacher records their discussions. When students do not use Standard American English, the teacher can model proper grammar, usage, punctuation, spelling and other conventions by recording the students' reports and observations in Standard American English. Students who see their own words presented this way will be exposed to the different syntax and other elements of Standard usage as it is applied to their own spoken dialects. This will help them absorb and remember Standard conventions more readily and will reinforce the concept of how Standard usage facilitates communication in groups of people who might otherwise use varying dialects of English.

When holding discussions in the classroom or while practicing the Language Experience Approach (LEA), the teacher can help students by suggesting different ways to word statements students have expressed in non-standard English. The teacher can also "translate" students' statements, descriptions, and narratives into Standard usage so that students can see direct examples of standard syntax and how it differs from their usual dialects. Teachers should be careful to engage in these activities in a non-judgmental way and discourage mocking or teasing of students who use different dialects or have different accents. Teachers should also present Standard American English as an alternative form of expression rather than a substitute for the student's usual dialect.

Speech

There are a number of elements to spoken language aside from grammar, syntax, and usage that should be addressed in the elementary classroom. These elements include:
- Pronunciation - Students often need help determining proper pronunciation, especially if they have only read a word and have never heard it spoken.
- Inflection - Inflection, or the stresses placed on individual words, can affect the meaning of a word or sentence.
- Tone - The tone of voice used can make a big difference in how a sentence is interpreted. Speech can be heard as polite, belligerent, or sarcastic based on the tone.
- Volume - Different volumes of speech are appropriate in different circumstances, such as talking to a friend in a small room versus addressing a crowd in a large auditorium.

Running record

A teacher keeps a running record when he or she observes a child reading aloud and makes notations about problems encountered during the exercise. The teacher can keep a running record of:
- Words the child mispronounces
- Words the child skips while reading
- Words the child repeats while reading
- Words the child does not understand

The teacher can take notes on another copy of the text including the way the child says each mispronounced word and which words are skipped, repeated, or not understood. This gives the teacher a better understanding of where the child's skills need improvement and can show this improvement when records are compared over time.

Informal assessment

Informal assessment often consists simply of observing students as they read, write and communicate. A teacher can gain a great deal of information this way and this is actually one of the best ways to assess a child's development in the elementary years. This type of assessment typically consists of portfolios or narratives about the child's performance rather than standardized testing or letter grades. Watching how a child responds to various tasks and expected work can also play a part in this type of assessment. If children are frustrated with certain tasks, they most likely need assistance in those areas. Informal assessment should be natural rather than performed in an artificial environment and should be continual rather than limited to a certain time period.

Clay's procedure for assessing if a child is ready to begin learning to read

In 1985, Clay proposed an approach to determine a child's understanding of books in general: how they work and what their different parts are. A typical and informal assessment, according to Clay's approach, is to ask the child where the title of the book is, where the child would begin reading, and where the text ends. The assessment could also establish whether the child understands the directionality of print (i.e., that English is read from left to right). A child who demonstrates an understanding of these basic concepts is displaying a readiness to learn to read.

Miscue analysis

When keeping a running record of a child's reading skill, the teacher keeps track of what words are skipped, repeated, mispronounced, or unfamiliar. The teacher then looks at the missed words and determines why the child had trouble with them. This analysis can reveal patterns in the child's reading, such as transposed letters, dropping of certain sounds, families of sounds that are not pronounced correctly, or other problems. This assessment of the child's mistakes is called a miscue analysis. Evaluating the miscues can help the teacher determine how he or she can assist the student in reading more accurately and can even help diagnose some reading disabilities, such as dyslexia or speech impediments.

Listening skills

In addition to reading, writing and speaking skills, elementary students should learn listening skills. This can involve listening to the teacher, paying attention to instructions, and listening to other students during specific activities. Students should learn to:
- Pay attention
- Maintain eye contact while being spoken to
- Be quiet while others are speaking
- Form responses so that the speaker knows the listener is listening

These skills can be interpreted as social skills but are also important to ensure a successful academic career. Students who know how to pay attention and follow

- 24 -

directions in class will continue to do well in upper elementary grades and secondary education.

Instant words

In 1957, Edward Fry put together a list of words he called instant words. He followed this up in 1980 with the "New Instant Word List." Fry considered these words to be those used most frequently in the English language. Students learning to read need to know these words as early as possible. From these words, students can learn additional words that are either variations on the instant word list or are combinations of words from this list. Teachers can make use of the list to assess students' language skills. If they can read these words without struggle, they are developing appropriate reading comprehension and will likely be able to tackle more advanced texts without undo difficulty.

Retelling a story

One of the best ways to determine if a child has understood a story is to ask him to retell it. Retelling is a valuable form of informal assessment and can be performed in a casual, one-on-one approach, journaling, or more formal conversations. Children can retell stories directly to the teacher or can be asked to narrate something they have read to the classroom or study group. They could also be asked to create artwork based on the story, provide a short book report or journal entry, or retell the story in another way that will keep the student engaged and interested in the material.

Readability graph

Developed by Edward Fry, the readability graph offers a mathematical equation to assess texts according to their grade level. The graph measures how many sentences are found in the text and the number of syllables for each one hundred words. These two values are graphed to determine the book's grade level. Using the readability graph can help teachers assign books appropriate to students' skill levels. Those with more advanced reading skills can be assigned books at a higher grade level than those who are still developing reading fluency.

Mathematics

Successful math instruction

Though mathematics instruction necessarily focuses on a certain amount of memorization, such as the multiplication tables and basic addition and subtraction facts, it also requires more complex approaches and use of higher level thinking skills. Major elements of a successful math curriculum include:

- Deductive reasoning
- Adaptive reasoning
- Inductive reasoning
- Analysis skills (upper levels of Bloom's Taxonomy)

In order to ensure students exercise all of these skills, teachers must use several approaches to instruction. Teachers must also be sure the curriculum builds upon previously learned concepts and leads logically into concepts presented in succeeding grades.

Presenting lectures

Several guidelines can help the lecture approach work more effectively for elementary students. These include:

- Keep lectures short to avoid boredom
- Use numerous visual aids to increase engagement and enhance understanding
- Be sure visual aids include pictures, drawings, and graphs to help visual learners
- Keep pictures, drawings or diagrams simple and straightforward

Although the lecture approach can be structured to appeal to auditory and visual learners, it is more difficult to engage kinesthetic learners through this method. Lectures should never be the sole or even the major means of presenting information to students at the elementary level. They should instead be used in conjunction with a variety of other methods to ensure student engagement and to appeal to different learning styles.

Mastery lecture

In a mastery lecture approach, the instructor lectures students by simply presenting facts and information in a formal atmosphere. Although this is a common approach in upper level grades and college instruction, it is not always the best method to use in elementary level instruction. A large amount of information can be presented in a short amount of time using the mastery lecture, but younger children are often bored by this approach and do not retain the information presented. It is also much more difficult to engage students during a lecture, especially if the lecture is too complex or long.

Note-taking skills

Note-taking is a skill that will serve children well throughout their educational career and beyond, particularly for lecture presentations. For this reason, it is important that students learn to take effective notes. Taking notes during a lecture or presentation can also help students remain more engaged with the material and as well as reinforcing the ideas presented in the lecture. The act of taking notes can help kinesthetic learners absorb the lecture material more effectively. In addition, if the student learns to express concepts in his or her own words in the process of taking notes, it can help increase understanding.

Teachers can employ several methods to teach effective note-taking. Some of these methods include:
- The teacher can model note-taking by taking her own notes on a white board or overhead during a lecture or presentation.
- The teacher can present students with a summary or outline of the presentation, showing how the information can be broken down into meaningful notes.
- The teacher can display the use of thinking maps, webs, or fishbone diagrams to organize notes.

In order to effectively implement these strategies, the teacher must plan ahead and assemble materials such as outlines or diagrams before the material is presented. In addition to helping the students learn to take notes, this organized approach can also result in a more effective lecture.

Deductive reasoning

Deductive reasoning involves applying generalized concepts to specific applications. In mathematics, this usually involves the student learning a general rule then practicing that rule in solving specific math problems that require the student to correctly apply that rule. The teacher can present the general rule, often through a lecture or presentation, and then provide practice problems that involve specific use of that rule. For example, the teacher could present rules of addition, then present practice problems and/or word problems. In the course of solving these problems, students will learn how the general rule applies to numerous specific examples.

Inductive reasoning

Inductive reasoning is the opposite of deductive reasoning in that students are shown specific examples and must then determine the generalized rule that applies to them. By watching the teacher perform multiple problems that use a specific rule, students can see how the rule is applied and thus determine how it can be generalized to apply to a wide variety of problems. For example, the teacher might demonstrate addition rules by performing a number of addition problems as demonstrations. The students will then work out the generalized version of the rule so that they can then solve the similar problems. Combining deductive and inductive reasoning techniques helps reinforce generalized rules and how they are applied to specific situations.

Inquiry lesson

In an inquiry lesson the teacher presents a question and students must work to determine the answer using inductive reasoning techniques. Typical structure of an inquiry lesson is:
1. The teacher presents the question.
2. Students brainstorm, listing everything they know regarding the presented topic.
3. Students separate what they already know into categories.
4. Students research specific topics within these categories.
5. Students present their research findings to the class.

The teacher will facilitate the process by providing support and resources, but the students are responsible for learning the concepts. By presenting their research at the end of the inquiry lesson, students are participating in a deductive learning approach in which they present the other students with the generalized rules they have learned from the inquiry.

The teacher must take a slightly different role in an inquiry lesson than in a more traditional lesson. His or her role can involve:
- Preparing the lesson
- Determining the most important information to learn from the lesson
- Providing resources
- Providing guidance
- Planning the lesson outcome

The teacher's role in preparing an inquiry lesson is vital, since the more prepared the teacher is the more successful the students will be. Preparation, prediction of results, and overall planning of resources, execution and environment are all important to a successful outcome in an inquiry lesson.

Inquiry lessons present numerous advantages in that they encourage students to use higher-level thinking skills. Inquiry lessons also tend to increase student engagement, keeping them motivated and interested in the topic they are exploring. This approach is much more active than other teaching methods, such as lecturing, where the students are expected to take in information passively. Teachers can also find inquiry lessons to be more interesting than traditional approaches, since lessons are never exactly the same. This helps the teacher engage with the material with higher level thinking, helping him or her teach better and more enthusiastically.

The major disadvantage to an inquiry lesson approach is the amount of time it takes to prepare as well as the amount of time it takes to execute. Teachers must do more—and more complex—preparation for inquiry lessons than for more traditional approaches. Students must also have more time to do the necessary research required for an inquiry lesson. Teachers and students must both have access to a wide range of resources in order for an inquiry lesson to be effective. Lastly, students who are not yet ready for the higher level thinking skills required for inquiry lessons might not benefit from this approach as much as their more advanced classmates.

Different teaching approaches

Depending upon the type of teaching approach a teacher chooses to use, his or her role will be slightly different. For example, if the teacher delivers material in a lecture, he is simply providing information to his students. Monitoring group discussions or evaluating papers and projects puts the teacher into the role of an active observer. Collaborative efforts in the classroom require the teacher to act as a facilitator or coach, helping students perform activities and reach their own conclusions rather than simply supplying information. The teacher must also provide resources in this role, adding an element of information provider to the collaborative effort.

As the teacher employs different teaching techniques, the student must take on different roles in order for the learning experience to be successful. Students participating in a discussion group, for instance, must become active listeners, willing to give and take constructive criticism and to provide ideas and questions to keep the discussion going. During a lecture session, students are more passive as they receive information, but can take a more active role by taking notes that help them engage. In collaboration scenarios, the student must be aware of the roles of different people in the group. At times the student must put his or her own interests aside for the good of the group, or allow another student to take control.

Adaptive reasoning

Adaptive reasoning in mathematics requires the student to think logically. This includes reasoning regarding concepts and how they apply to specific situations. A student can then evaluate an answer to a problem based on its reasonableness. For example, if a student adds two numbers together and the result is smaller than any one of those two numbers, the student can use adaptive reasoning to determine that this is not a reasonable answer. Adaptive reasoning is particularly important when children are doing word problems in mathematics. Converting the elements of the word problem into numbers, concepts and specific operations requires use of adaptive thinking and an ability to judge the reasonableness of a particular operation or a particular solution.

Bloom's Taxonomy amd mathematics

Analysis is the fourth level of Bloom's Taxonomy, which consists of six levels overall. It is considered a higher level skill. Analysis allows students to examine a mathematic word problem and determine how to use the information within the word problem to construct a reasonable mathematical approach that will solve the problem. The student must analyze the contents of the problem, apply concepts learned regarding mathematical operations and functions, and use this information to solve the problem. However, analysis is not the only level of Bloom's Taxonomy used in teaching and learning mathematics. All levels of the taxonomy should be considered during lesson development and are used during student learning.

Scope, sequence, and the seven major categories of math instruction

The scope of a curriculum is defined as the major topics that will be covered. The sequence of the curriculum is the order in which these topics are presented. In mathematics, the scope and sequence are very similar in each state in the US. The major topics covered in elementary mathematics instruction are:
1. Numbers, order and values
2. Addition and subtraction
3. Fractions and comparisons
4. Multiplication and division
5. Ratios, measurements and decimals
6. Graphing, estimation and solving problems
7. Colors, equations and geometry

These subjects are covered in increasing detail and difficulty as children go through elementary school grades.

Number concepts

Students in elementary grades must learn to relate numbers to quantities of objects. In addition to the concept that numbers refer to quantities, students will also learn:
- Counting numbers vs. whole numbers - Whole numbers are the same as counting numbers, with 0 added at the beginning of the sequence.
- Numbers vs. numerals - A number is the concept of a quantity of objects, while a numeral is a symbol representing a quantity.
- Skip counting - This includes counting by twos, threes, counting only even or odd numbers, or counting by other multiples.
- Odd vs. even numbers - Even numbers can be divided by two; odd numbers cannot.

Expanded notation and exponential notation

Expanded notation is a way to visually demonstrate place value. The number is expanded to show the value of each individual digit. For example, the number 42 in expanded notation would be represented as (4 x 10) + (2 x 1). This shows the exact value of each digit: 4 x 10 represents 40, and 2 x 1 represents a quantity of 2, so 42 is equivalent to 40 + 2. Exponential notation is similar, but uses exponents to express the values. In the above example, the exponential notation would be (4 x 10^1) + (2 x 10^0). The number 562 would be expressed as (5 x 10^2) + (6 x 10^1) + (2 x 10^0).

Sets

In mathematics, the concept of sets involves groupings of items that are similar in some way. Actions that can be performed on sets and the individual members of a set include:
- Comparing objects to each other
- Classifying objects according to a specific criteria
- Sorting objects according to a pattern (patterning)
- Sorting objects according to size (ordering)

Students can also practice oral counting by counting the number of objects in different categories.

Base-10 and place value

Base-10 represents the system of numeration used in the US and elsewhere. The base-10 numeration system also determines the place value of numbers. In numbers with more than one digit, each digit is ten times the value of the digit to its immediate right, or one-tenth the value of the digit to its immediate left. The concept of place value is vital to understanding the value of numerals and how they are used to represent actual quantities. Students can learn place value by isolating specific digits in a number and explaining what the actual value of that numeral is according to its place value.

Mathematical operations

Mathematical operations are actions taken upon groups of numbers. The four operations are:
1. Addition
2. Subtraction
3. Multiplication
4. Division

Addition occurs when numbers are combined, producing a new numerical total. This total is referred to as a sum. The form in which addition is expressed, also called an algorithm, consists of two addends and the sum. As a binary function, addition only combines two numbers in each operation. Subtraction is the opposite, or inverse, function to addition. Also a binary operation, subtraction removes one value from another to produce the difference between those two numbers. The subtraction algorithm consists of a minuend, from which a subtrahend is subtracted to produce the difference.

Multiplication and division are also inverse functions to each other, just as addition and subtraction are. Multiplication is simply a shorthand way of performing multiple addition operations. The answer to a multiplication problem is called the product. Division is the opposite of multiplication, and functions as a shorthand method of performing multiple subtraction operations. The answer to a division problem is referred to as the quotient.

Regrouping in addition and subtraction

Regrouping in addition and subtraction involves reassigning values from one place value to another. In addition, regrouping was previously referred to as "carrying." When the sum of two numbers in the ones place results in a sum larger than ten, the group of ten is regrouped into the tens place, and so on.

In subtraction, regrouping was previously referred to as "borrowing." If the number in the ones place in the subtrahend (the bottom or second number) is larger than the number in the ones place of the minuend (the top or first number), values from the tens place are regrouped to the ones place. The number in the minuend is then increased by a quantity of ten.
The best way to present the concept of regrouping to elementary students is through concrete modeling.

Commutative property, associative property, and distributive property

Three major properties affecting multiplication include:
- Commutative Property - The commutative property states that the order of the factors does not affect the final solution. For example, 2 x 4 is the same as 4 x 2.
- Associative Property - The associative property involves grouping numbers in problems involving three or more factors or addends. For example, (2 x 4) x 3 is the same as 2 x (4 x 3).

- Distributive Property - The distributive property states that a larger number can be expressed as a sum of two numbers and when each of these two numbers is multiplied by the same factor, the products can be added together to achieve the solution. For example, to solve 104 x 11, you can multiple 11 x 100 (getting 1,100), then 4 x 11(getting 44). 1,100 + 44 = 1,144, which is the product of 104 x 11.

Modeling mathematical operations

Modeling mathematical operations is the best way to present these concepts to students. The four major ways to model mathematical operations are:
1. Concrete - Excellent for kinesthetic learners, the concrete method provides real objects for the students to use. These are often referred to as manipulatives. Concrete modeling helps the students relate the symbols of a math problem to actual objects.
2. Semiconcrete - Instead of using manipulatives, students use illustrations of actual objects.
3. Abstract - The actual objects or pictures of objects are replaced with numerals to represent them.
4. Semiabstract - One object in the operation is replaced with a numeral while the other object is still represented by a picture or another, more visual representation.

Modeling the operation of multiplication

Multiplication can be modeled in the classroom using concrete objects divided into groups. For example, 2 x 2 can be modeled by showing the students two groups of two objects. Concrete modeling helps students understand the ideas behind mathematical operations more clearly and relate the symbols used in mathematics to actual objects and manipulations performed upon those objects.

In addition, graphical representations, such as arrays, can be useful to show students a more concrete example of multiplication and how it works.

Property of reciprocals and the multiplicative identity property of 1

The property of reciprocals states that any number multiplied by its reciprocal results in a product of 1. The reciprocal of a number is defined as one divided by that number. The reciprocal is usually expressed as a fraction. For example, 2 x ½ = 1, and 4 x ¼ = 1.

The multiplicative identity property of 1 states that if a number is multiplied by 1, the product is the original number. For example, 2 x 1 = 2, and 4 x 1 = 4.

Multiples

Multiples are defined as the products that are derived when any given number is multiplied by the counting numbers. For example, 2 x 1, 2 x 2, 2 x 3, etc. will produce the multiples of 2 as 2, 4, 6, and so on to infinity.

In multiplication, regrouping is used in much the same way as it is in addition. If the product of two numbers in the ones place in a multiplication problem is greater than 10, the multiples of 10 in the product are shifted to the tens place. As with regrouping in addition, this is most easily understood by most students if it is presented in a concrete fashion.

Factors, prime numbers and composite numbers

Factors - The factors of a number are those numbers that can be divided evenly into that number. Conversely, pairs of factors can be multiplied to produce the number. For example, 2 x 3 and 6 x 1 are both equal to 6. The factors of 6, then, are 1, 2, 3, and 6.

Prime numbers - Prime numbers only have two factors: the number itself and 1. For example, the only numbers that can be multiplied together to make a product of 5 are 5 and 1. This means 5 is a prime number.

Composite numbers - Composite numbers have more than two factors. In the example above, 6 is broken down into four factors; therefore 6 is a composite number.

Rational numbers, fractions, decimals and percents

Rational numbers - Numbers that can be expressed as a fraction (x/y), in which both x and y are integers and y is never 0. A rational number can also be expressed as a decimal or as a percent.

Fractions - Numbers expressed in the form x/y. Both x and y must be whole numbers. Fractions cannot always be translated into integers. However, all integers can be translated into fractions.

Decimals - Another way of representing fractions in the base ten system; each place to the right of the decimal point decreases in value by a factor of ten.

Percent - Expresses a fraction as a portion of 100. For example, 25% represents 25 out of 100 units, or 25/100.

Special properties of 0 and of 1

The numbers 0 and 1 have special properties related to multiplication and addition. These properties are:
- Identity element of addition - If 0 is added to any number, the result is that number. In other words, the number's identity or value remains the same.
- Multiplication property of 0 - If any number is multiplied by 0, the product is always 0.
- Identity element of multiplication - If any number is multiplied by 1, the result is the original number. The number's identity or value remains the same.

There is no identity element for subtraction because the commutative property does not apply to subtraction. 0 cannot be considered an identity element for division because numbers cannot be divided by 0.

Modeling division

Division can be modeled in two different ways: measurement division and partitive division. In measurement division, students are told how many objects there are in all, how many objects are in each individual set, and must determine the number of sets. In partitive division, the student knows the total and the number of sets and must determine the number of objects in each set. Using concrete modeling makes this process easier for most students, especially at the elementary level.

Ratios and proportions

Fractions can also be expressed as ratios. For example, the fraction ½ can be expressed as the ratio 1:2, or spelled out as "the ratio of 1 to 2." In ratios, the emphasis is upon the relationship between the two numbers.

A proportion is an equation that presents two equal ratios. The student might be asked to provide a missing number from one of the ratios. For example, a proportion might be expressed as ½=2/4. For a student to solve the proportion, one number will be substituted with a variable: $1/x=2/4$.

Angle, vertex and degrees

An angle is represented by two lines joined at one end. The lines are often ended with arrows, indicating they continue on into infinity. The point at which the lines or arrows are joined is called the vertex.

Angles are measured with a unit called the degree, expressed as °. A full circle consists of 360 degrees, or 360°. An angle is measured based on the portion of a full circle it would make up if its vertex were located at the circle's center.

Ways lines can relate to each other

A line connects two points and is a one-dimensional construct. Lines can relate to each other in three ways:
1. Intersecting lines - Two lines that cross each other at any single point are seen to intersect. The intersection of lines produces angles of varying sizes.
2. Perpendicular lines - Lines are considered perpendicular if their vertex forms a right, or 90°, angle.
3. Parallel lines - Parallel lines do not intersect, nor will they ever intersect no matter how far they are extended in either direction on the same plane.

Perimeter, area and volume

The perimeter is the distance around a two-dimensional object. It is determined by adding the lengths of all the sides of the object.

Area represents the space within a two-dimensional object. For example, the amount of carpet used to cover a floor is determined by calculating the area of the floor. Area is determined by multiplication and is expressed as a unit of measurement squared, such as square feet or square inches.

Volume represents the space contained within a three-dimensional object. It is also determined by multiplication and is expressed as a cubed unit, such as cubic feet or cubic inches.

Complementary angles, supplementary angles, vertical angles, and transversals

Complimentary angles consist of two angles whose measurements add up to 90°. For example, a set of two 45° angles, or of one 30° angle and one 60° angle, would both be considered sets of complementary angles.

Supplementary angles are two angles whose measurements total 180°. If placed back to back, the bases of these angles would form a straight line.

Two intersecting lines form two sets of vertical angles. Vertical angles are situated opposite from each other, with a shared vertex, and measure the same number of degrees.

If a single line crosses two or more other lines, that line is known as a transversal. Transversals create sets of interior and exterior angles.

Triangles and the Pythagorean Theorem

Triangles have several major properties. In any given triangle, the sum of the three angles will always equal 180°. Using this property, students can determine the value of one angle if the values of the other two angles are supplied.

The Pythagorean Theorem applies only to right triangles. A right angle consists of two lines whose vertex produces a 90° angle. A longer, third line connects these two lines to form the longest side, or hypotenuse, of the triangle. The Pythagorean Theorem states that in any right triangle, the sum of the squares of the two short sides will be the same as the square of the hypotenuse. It is expressed formulaically as $a^2 + b^2 = c^2$.

Polygons

Polygons are two-dimensional constructs formed by the intersection of at least three straight lines. Rectangles, triangles, pentagons and quadrilaterals are all polygons.

Since the intersection of lines always forms an angle, polygons enclose numerous angles. The number of angles in a polygon is determined by its number of sides. For example, a triangle encloses three angles, while a quadrilateral (four-sided polygon) encloses four angles.

A regular polygon encloses angles that are all equal to each other. A rectangle or a square consists of lines that all meet at 90° angles. An equilateral triangle is also a regular polygon, with each angle equal to 60°.

Symmetry, similarity, scaling, and translation

Symmetry refers to objects that can be divided into two identical figures with a single line. Regular polygons such as squares and rectangles are symmetrical. So are circles.

Similarity refers to objects that are shaped the same but are of different sizes. A 2 x 2 foot square is similar to a 4 x 4 foot square even though one is half the size of the other.

Transformation involves changing a geometrical object in various ways. This can include scaling, turning, sliding, or even flipping the object.

Scaling involves transforming an object by making it larger or smaller. Scaling is uniform in all directions and results in an object similar to the original, based on the geometric definition of "similar."

Networks and building three-dimensional objects

A network, also called a net, consists of a number of points that are connected by straight lines. The points are referred to as the vertices, or nodes, of the figure. The lines are called arcs. These patterns of points connected by lines serve as patterns from which three-dimensional figures can be constructed. These figures can include cubes, spheres, pyramids or other figures.

Networks themselves can be drawn out on a piece of paper by the teacher. The student can then cut out the network and determine how it must be folded and where the sides must be attached in order to form the desired geometrical figure. Networks create a concrete means for students to comprehend how three-dimensional figures are structured.

Mode, median, mean and range

Mode, median, mean and range are ways of describing characteristics of a set of numbers.
- Mode - The number that occurs most often in a set of numbers.
- Mean - The sum of the numbers in a set divided by how many numbers are in the set.
- Median - The number in the middle when placed in sequential order. Half the numbers will be smaller than the median and half will be larger. If the set contains an odd number of numbers, the median will exist in the set. For a set with an even number of members, the median is found by averaging the two numbers in the center.
- Range - The range of values covered in the set. To determine the range, subtract the set's smallest number from the set's largest number.

Ordered pairs and the coordinate plane

Ordered pairs are a way of representing the location of a specific point on a plane. The coordinate plane divides the plane into four quadrants. The coordinate plane is used to create ordered pairs by serving as a reference point from which to define the location of the point or points.

The coordinate plane consists of perpendicular lines that intersect at the origin. This intersection defines the plane's center. The horizontal line in a coordinate plane is referred to as the x-axis while the vertical line is called the y-axis. Ordered pairs represent the distance of a point from the origin of the coordinate plane, by indicating where the point is located on the x- and the y-axis of the plane.

Common systems of measurement

A system of measurement is the overall system used to measure length, weight, or volume. The two major systems of measurement used in the US are:

1. US system of measurement - Also called the English system, it consists of familiar units of length such as inches feet, yards and miles. Ounces and pounds are used for weight, while units of volume include cups, pints and gallons.

2. Metric system of measurement - The metric system is based on base-10, making it more consistent and sometimes even more accurate. It consists of basic units of measurement to which prefixes are added to indicate larger or smaller units according to the base-10 structure.

Probability

Probability refers to the likelihood that a given event will take place. It is determined by the number of times the event could possibly take place divided by the number of all the possible outcomes. For example, if one buys two lottery tickets from a pool of three million tickets, the probability of that person's tickets winning is 2/3,000,000. If a bag contains four blue balls and seven green balls, the probability of pulling a blue ball from the bag is 4/11. This represents the number of blue balls divided by the total number of balls. The probability of pulling out a green ball is 7/11.

Problem-solving strategies

In addition to teaching specific operations, mathematics teachers should be sure students learn strategies that can be used to solve problems. Some of these strategies include:

- Estimating
- Using a chart or table to parse the problem
- Finding patterns that offer clues to solving the problem
- Organizing the information from the problem into a list
- Drawing a picture to provide a graphic representation of the problem
- Guessing, then check the guess to judge its accuracy
- Working the problem backwards, beginning with the result
- Translating the problem into a mathematical equation using unknowns
- Acting the problem out
- Working a problem that is similar, but simpler, to the problem presented

Solving word problems

In order to successfully solve a word problem, a student must be able to translate the problem into mathematical terms. The first and most important step in this process is determining the right operation. For example, the student must be able to determine if a particular problem is best solved by adding or subtracting. The major ways for a student to determine the appropriate operation for a word problem are:

- Key words - The student can look for key words in the problem such as "removed from," "divided," or "taken away from."
- Reasonableness - The student must be able to determine if a particular operation is reasonable given the parameters of the problem.
- Formal and informal evaluation - The student should be able to break the problem down in both formal and informal ways to determine the most appropriate operation.

Technology in the mathematics classroom

Technology has become so pervasive in our society that it must be considered as an important part of the classroom experience. Advantages of technology include:

- Provides a way to present information in ways that appeal to a variety of learning styles
- Helps keep students engaged
- Provides a wider range of perspectives for students of different backgrounds
- Helps the teacher organize his or her lessons and records more efficiently

Disadvantages can include:

- Technological "crutches" such as calculators and computers can become a substitute for actual learning
- Learning how to use the technology could detract from learning the subject being taught
- Students who are accustomed to using technology at home will have an advantage over those who are not

Types of technology that can be used to great effect in the mathematics classroom include:

- Calculators
- Computers
- Overheads
- Videos
- Filmstrips
- Smartboards
- Spreadsheets
- Presentation software
- Graphics programs

The teacher's individual teaching style as well as the needs of the students in an individual classroom should determine what technological approaches are used in the classroom. Teaching style will also play a large role in determining what technology will be effective in enhancing the learning experience for the students and the teaching experience for the teacher.

Science

Scientific method

The scientific method provides a framework by which theories can be tested through prediction, hypotheses, experimentation, and interpretation of resulting data. It should be presented, taught and practiced as a process that can change from one situation to another, but that still follows certain guidelines to preserve the accuracy and relevance of results. Performing scientific inquiry according to the scientific method also enables different scientists to communicate with each other using a shared vocabulary so that they can understand each other's results and build upon each other's work.

Using the scientific method requires students to articulate their understanding of scientific concepts. Adherence and understanding of the scientific method can be used as a means of assessing how well a student has understood a specific concept.

Scientific observation and experimentation

Five steps vital to the scientific method and to any experimentation performed in a science classroom are as follows:
1. Observe - Determining an occurrence that can be measured via experimentation
2. Organize - Placing data in a cohesive form
3. Predict - Stating the expected result of an experiment before performing that experiment
4. Infer - Use existing information to infer additional information
5. Experiment - Test a single variable in a controlled experimental environment where only that variable is independent

Using these five elements helps students adhere to the scientific method in order to produce relevant results in the classroom. How a student predicts the outcome of an experiment can also serve as an assessment of his or her understanding of scientific concepts.

Hypothesis and planning an experiment

A hypothesis is a type of prediction. Before performing an experiment, the student considers the variables that are to be tested and makes a prediction about how these variables will relate to each other. The experiment is then designed to determine the validity of the hypothesis. A hypothesis must be clearly defined and testable in order to result in a successful experiment. The four major steps in planning a scientific experiment are:

1. Identify variables relevant to the experiment
2. Decide what tools will work best to measure these variables and record results
3. Remove any variables that could adversely affect the outcome of the experiment
4. Determine the best way to evaluate the resulting data

Tools used in scientific experiments, observation, and inquiry

Major tools used in the science classroom enable students to make observations beyond what they can observe with the naked eye. These tools include:

- Microscope - Used to observe objects too small to see with the naked eye
- Telescope - Used to observe objects too distant to see in detail with the naked eye
- Spectroscope - Breaks beams of light down into individual colors
- Spectrophotometer - Determines how much of each color is absorbed and uses this information to determine what substance is being observed.

In addition to these tools, mathematics is an important tool in scientific observation and inquiry. Mathematics allows students to evaluate results and determine their relevance. Math is also often employed in making predictions about the outcome of an experiment.

Inquiry method

The inquiry method is another way to present scientific concepts to an elementary classroom. The inquiry method can be presented in one of two ways:

1. Inductive method - Students perform research and gather data from which they form generalizations and rules.
2. Deductive method - Students are presented with generalizations and rules, and then find specific examples of these rules through research.

The inquiry method encourages students to employ higher level thinking skills. In inquiry lessons, the teacher facilitates learning, but students must do their own research and projects in order to learn the specific concepts being presented. Inquiry lessons require preparation and work on the part of the teacher, who must ensure the goals of the lesson are clearly defined and that sufficient resources are available.

Earth science concepts

Several concepts are important to the study of geology, or the structure of the Earth:
- Earth consists of a solid core, a semi-molten mantle and a solid crust.
- The Earth's crust is divided into large sections called plates, which move on the surface of the mantle.
- The movement of the crust causes faults, earthquakes and volcanoes. Study of this movement is called plate tectonics.
- More gradual movement of the plates, called continental drift, shifts the size and position of continents. This movement can also produce mountain ranges, or result in continued growth of existing mountain ranges.
- New crust is created at certain locations in the ocean, called mid-ocean ridges. This crust moves away from its origin point in a process called seafloor spreading.

Revolution of the Earth and the tilt of the Earth on its axis

Major concepts in earth science include:
- The Earth revolves around the sun.
- The Earth is tilted on its axis.
- Earth's revolution around the sun and the tilt of the Earth on its axis cause the change of seasons.
- Summer occurs when a particular area is closer to the sun.
- Winter occurs when a particular area is farther from the sun.
- Summer and winter occur during opposite times of the year in the Northern and Southern hemispheres.
- Because the Earth is tilted on its axis, days are longer in the summer and shorter in the winter. Each year includes a longest day, a shortest day, and two days in which night and day are of equal length (equinoxes).

Matter

Matter itself is defined as anything having both mass and volume. Mass determines the quantity of matter in a specific object. Volume is the space that the object takes up. Other properties of matter include:
- Weight - The gravitational force exerted upon an object.
- Density - The mass of an object as compared to its volume.

Matter can undergo physical or chemical changes. Physical changes affect the shape or size of an object without changing its molecular structure. Chemical changes alter the molecular structure. In chemical reactions, a substance can combine with another substance or break apart to form a new substance.

Elements

Matter is classified into several categories:
- Compounds - A substance formed by combining different elements in exact proportions
- Elements - Substances consisting of a single type of atom
- Mixtures - Substances that are mixed together, but the individual molecules remain separate, mixtures are considered homogenous due to this even distribution.
- Solutions - A substance in which one substance is evenly distributed in another substance.

Matter can also exist in three states:
1. Gas - Does not have a definite volume or a defined shape; is the least dense of the states of matter
2. Liquid - Does not have a definite shape but the volume can be measured
3. Solid - Maintains a consistent volume and shape; the densest of the states of matter.

Metabolic processes of plants

Metabolism refers to the group of activities a living being must perform in order to support its necessary activities. Plants perform the following certain functions that define them as plants:
- Photosynthesis - Plants make use of sunlight to create energy in special cells call chloroplasts. A green pigment within plant cells called chlorophyll reacts to sunlight to facilitate this process.
- Respiration - Plants exchange gases by releasing oxygen and absorbing carbon dioxide during the process of photosynthesis.
- Reproduction - Plants can reproduce sexually or asexually. Asexual reproduction only requires a single cell, while sexual reproduction requires the joining of two different, specialized cells.
- Transpiration - This is the release of water from plants through their leaves.

Biogeochemical cycles that function within the environment

Several cycles function within the environment in order to maintain life. These cycles consist of interactions between biological and geological elements.

Nitrogen cycle - This cycle ensures that the air maintains the proper amount of nitrogen to sustain life. Nitrogen-fixing bacteria in the soil help convert nitrogen from the air into a form of nitrogen plants are able to use. Nitrifying bacteria convert animal waste to nitrogen that returns to the soil. De-nitrifying bacteria convert dead animals and dead plants into nitrogen that returns to the atmosphere.

Carbon dioxide-oxygen cycle - This cycle occurs when plants take in carbon dioxide to produce energy and release oxygen as a waste product. Animals then take in the oxygen to produce energy and release carbon dioxide as a waste product.

Biology

Biology is the branch of science that studies living objects. In order to be considered living, a creature must perform all of the following activities at some point during its lifetime:
1. Respire, or breathe
2. Excrete waste
3. Grow
4. Move
5. Respond
6. Reproduce
7. Secrete chemicals that help with the other necessary activities that define life
8. Repair itself
9. Actively acquire food

Living things are made up of cells. A single cell is considered a living thing and some living things consist of only one cell. Others consist of numerous cells working together to perform all the different activities required to sustain life. In multi-cellular organisms, individual cells are specialized to perform specific functions within the organism.

Animals

Animals are made up of specialized cells that group together to form tissues; these tissues group together to form organs; these groups of organs form a system; and each system within an animal performs a specific function. The systems that make up animals are:
- Skeletal - Supports the body; made of bones as well as ligaments and cartilage
- Muscular - Controls bodily movement, both voluntary and involuntary
- Nervous - Sends signals that stimulate bodily movement, both voluntary and involuntary; includes the brain, which evaluates and interprets these signals.
- Respiratory - Brings air and oxygen into the body
- Circulatory - Transports blood, which contains oxygen along with different nutrients and lymph, throughout the body
- Immune - Removes foreign bodies, such as viruses, from the body
- Digestive - Converts food into energy
- Excretory - Removes waste from the body

Laboratory equipment

Science classrooms have several types of equipment available to perform experiments and to facilitate various learning experiences. Students can evaluate an experiment based on the desired results in order to determine the best equipment to use to measure those results. Some guidance will be required at first to help students determine the suitability of certain equipment. They will also require guidance in how to use the equipment. After students acquire an understanding of how the equipment works and how to use it, they will be able to use equipment to confirm their own hypotheses and to independently develop questions and find the answers.

Safety procedures

Safety procedures are particularly important in a science lab or classroom. Among the procedures that should be observed are:
- Proper and regular use of safety equipment
- Proper and regular monitoring of chemicals
- Proper use and disposal of chemicals
- Proper storage of chemicals
- Fire prevention strategies and equipment
- Guidelines for handling living things

All these procedures should be implemented in the classroom. All students should also be aware of the proper procedures in case of any kind of accident. For example, if a student spills a chemical, he or she should know the proper procedure for cleanup. An important part of teaching science curriculum includes teaching, reviewing and enforcing safety procedures.

Technology

Technology such as microscopes, telescopes and other measuring equipment is vital to the science classroom because they are used in scientific experimentation. Technology can also help with presenting science concepts, gathering and organizing data, assessing student performance, and keeping track of class records as well as results of experiments. Students can use computers for research, to keep track of experiments, and to compose papers and other materials. Major types of software that can be integrated into the classroom include:
- Databases
- Spreadsheets
- Word processing programs
- Desktop publishing
- Online databases or cloud computing elements

- Internet browsers for research and/or communication
- Practice lessons or drills
- Tutorials

A variety of software can be used to help students demonstrate their understanding of scientific concepts. Programs that present straightforward testing experiences are the most obvious application. In addition, students can make use of graphics programs to draw pictures, diagrams, or graphs that demonstrate their understanding of specific concepts such as the structure and components of a plant cell. Programs presenting problems for the student to solve can stimulate higher level thinking and demonstrate the student's knowledge. Simulations can give students the opportunity to experience situations that would be difficult to present in a classroom setting due to time, cost, or other issues. The teacher can use any of these applications as a tool for assessment.

Internet safety

The Internet is an excellent resource for research and learning, but it can also present problems in a classroom. These problems can include:
- Viruses or spyware infiltrating the system
- Vulnerability of the school computer systems to hacking
- Exposure of students to inappropriate material
- Research that uncovers inaccurate information

In order to prevent issues from developing, the teacher should institute a set of rules regarding Internet use including:
- Ensure classroom use of material from the Internet is not in violation of copyright
- Install firewalls and virus protection in all computers
- Only allow specific, qualified personnel to install or uninstall software
- Install filters to prevent students from accessing inappropriate material

Help students learn to judge the accuracy and reliability of various Internet sources

Slide presentations

Slide presentations can work well for presenting information to the classroom, but certain guidelines, if followed, can help these presentations be more effective.
- Be sure the presentation is structured so that students will be able to follow it easily.
- Be sure students will be able to see the presentation and read it easily even from the back of the classroom.
- Be sure all necessary equipment works and is appropriate to the size of the classroom.
- Always focus on the main message of the presentation.

- Be sure the presentation is consistent in presentation. Fonts, backgrounds, colors and transitions should be the same throughout the presentation.
- Keep individual slides simple and not overly busy so the information is more easily absorbed.

Science and technology

Technology and science go hand in hand. Technology is the practical application of science. Science leads to the improvement of technology and more advanced technology allows us as a society to make additional discoveries in the field of science. Knowledge of science helps individuals understand and apply technology in ways that can improve their individual quality of life and even help improve conditions for the world population as a whole.

Some technology, however, can be detrimental to the environment, individuals, or communities. In these cases, science can help determine how the technology can be improved to reduce these detrimental effects.

Teachable questions

Teachable questions are those which can be easily demonstrated and which a student can easily prove he or she understands. In assessment, a teachable question has a clear-cut answer that the student can provide in order to demonstrate his knowledge of the subject. In planning scientific experiments, a teachable question is one that can be easily answered through experimentation. It also must present variables that can be measured accurately and adequately controlled during the course of the experiment.

Teachable questions are straightforward, well-defined, and have a single answer. If too many variables or too many possible answers are introduced, the experiment will not be successful or the student will not be able to demonstrate his knowledge of the subject being tested.

Social Studies

Social studies curriculum

The scope and sequence for social studies at the elementary level can differ from state to state, but the overall progression remains similar. A typical scope and sequence from Kindergarten through eighth grade is:

- Kindergarten — Immediate environment; topics cover home, family, and school
- First grade — Continued exploration of the immediate environment
- Second grade — Includes the local community
- Third grade — History and geography of the local state; can also include the history of the US and US holidays.
- Fourth grade — World regions and/or the history and geography of their state
- Fifth grade — Extended American history and geography
- Sixth grade — World history and world geography
- Seventh grade — More in-depth study of American history and/or state history
- Eighth grade — Continued exploration of American history and introduction of civics.

Systematic inquiry

Systematic inquiry requires students to gather information from several sources, organize it, and analyze it. Students can independently design and carry out their own inquiries or investigations to bring together information regarding specific issues in the field of social studies. Sources that can be employed in these investigations include:

- Primary sources - Sources written in the historical period being studied or by the historical figure being studied.
- Secondary sources - Sources written about the historical period or figure; including biographies, encyclopedias and historical texts.

Both types of sources are readily available in libraries, online, or other outlets. Students and teachers can use these sources to conduct investigations or set up lesson plans. Teachers should help students evaluate the validity of secondary sources.

Primary source documents

Primary source documents are among the most relevant and useful tools in social studies instruction. Using primary sources allows a student to obtain an intimate look into the thoughts and activities of people who were alive during the time being studied. Documents can include court records, census data, letters, diaries, music, or legal documents.

Primary source documents are more accessible than ever thanks to the Internet. The Library of Congress maintains a number of primary source documents online. In addition, many historical societies or organizations dedicated to a particular historical period also maintain online archives of primary source documents. Local museums or historical societies might have primary source documents available where students can actually look at them or, in some cases, read or handle them.

Local residents as resources

In early grades, social studies focuses on the local community. Members of the local community can serve as valuable resources for study, as can locations in the community. Individuals could also visit the classroom to present information about their jobs or roles in the community. For example, a lesson on fire departments could include a visit to a local fire station as well as interviews with the fire chief or other fire fighters. As with any lesson, those involving field trips or visits will be more successful if they are planned ahead and if the teacher has a clearly defined goal for the trip or visit. Visitors should also be aware of this lesson goal so that they can address topics relevant to the students' interests.

Geography

Geography is the study of places on the earth. It covers five main themes:
1. Location - Absolute vs. relative location used to identify where a specific landmark is found
2. Place - Names of states, cities, towns, countries and regions; includes political science
3. Movement and connections - How transportation and communication connect people all over the world and how these connections have grown and changed
4. Regions, processes and patterns - Includes variations in economy, climate, politics, and culture within specific regions, making each one unique; includes sociology, politics and economics
5. Human interaction with the environment - How human beings make use of, change, and are limited by the environment; includes ecology.

The past has a profound effect on the present, and determines the human component of an area develops and grows. The three major concepts involving this idea are:
- Human populations will modify an environment to meet their needs. This can lead either to improvement of the environment, or environmental destruction.

- Cultural factors are influenced by physical factors. The type of clothes, food, and shelter a particular group of people uses is determined largely by what is available in their environment.
- Changes occur constantly. Populations change the environment and the environment itself changes due to human and geological factors.

The growth of cities and even nations is based on the choice of specific areas for activities such as habitation, agriculture, transportation, and other activities. Several factors determine whether locations are suitable for these activities:
- Climate
- Altitude
- Presence of water
- Types of plants present
- Density of population
- Type of government
- Existing landforms

Any of these factors, or a combination thereof, will determine if a location is suitable for habitation or population expansion. As technology advances in an area, these factors can determine whether certain industries will be successful there.

Physical geography

Physical geography refers to the study of Earth's physical attributes. This can include landforms like mountains, rivers, deserts and plateaus; types of soil; climate, altitude and rainfall; and types and quantity of vegetation. It also includes the movement and position of the earth itself, as well as the makeup of its atmosphere. Physical geography can tell students a great deal about how the earth is made up and how various factors lead to the development of physical features on the earth, but it does not include how humans interact with these physical features.

Maps

Maps create a graphical representation of various portions of the Earth or, in the case of global maps, of the entire Earth. Map study generally begins with studying the globe to give students an understanding of the makeup of the Earth and where different regions are located. Other concepts included in map study are:
- Types of maps - Geologic, political, environmental, resource, topographical, themed, etc.
- Map key - Includes the compass rose, map scale, and legends that explain each of the symbols used on a particular map
- Measurement grids - Applicable mostly to globes, this includes latitude and longitude, the Equator, the Tropics of Cancer and Capricorn, parallels and meridians.

Cultural geography

Cultural geography discusses how humans and animals interact with their environment. Physical properties of the environment can affect various factors including:
- Types of vegetation available
- Types of animals that can survive
- How accessible an area is
- What kind of shelter is available
- What kinds of physical resources are available

The availability of important resources such as food, water, and shelter can determine whether or not a large human population can be sustained in a specific area. Physical geography that restricts growth of a population can keep certain settlements from growing. All of these factors are important to an understanding of a particular area or region and why it developed in the way it has.

Major regions of the world

The world can be divided into regions in a number of ways; one common way is the seven continents: Africa, Asia, Europe, North America, South America, Australia, and Antarctica. Another way is to discuss the Northern and Southern Hemispheres or the Eastern and Western Hemispheres. A discussion could also involve climatic regions, latitude or political divisions.
In the elementary classroom, students can compare and contrast these various regions by researching the areas and discovering ways in which they are similar and different. They can also compare social studies concepts to familiar concepts from other study areas, such as science, for higher-level thinking and analysis.

Sociology

The social interaction of human beings is quite complex. The science of sociology seeks to study the wide variety of social interaction that exists in human populations. Groups observed by sociologists include:
- Populations of cities or towns
- Families of various sizes
- Organizations
- Groups of the same gender
- Groups of similar ages
- Groups with specific characteristics such as similar occupations or racial characteristics

Sociologists also observe the way individuals interact with institutions, such as governments. These studies can help determine differences and similarities between individual groups and can help improve how these groups interact and communicate with each other.

Human population adaptation

The physical environment determines what types of activities are most suitable to a specific area. However, human populations can adapt to prosper in most environments by using clothing and shelter and by developing ways of procuring or producing food. In many cases, these activities lead to changes in the environment. For example, a human population might redirect a water source to enable them to grow food. This could lead to a reduction in water supplied to another area, causing local vegetation and animal populations to fluctuate or die out. More recently, humans have become more aware of the negative impacts of changing their environment and work harder to ensure that modifying the environment produces a less negative impact on existing animals, plants and physical structures.

Human populations often move from one area to another. Four major factors that lead to this movement are:
1. Physical - If a particular area does not provide the necessary resources or room for a population to thrive, that population may relocate.
2. Economic - Individuals, families, or groups might move to an area where their economic needs are better met or where the cost of living is lower. Some might move to areas with higher economic demands.
3. Political - Changes in a political system in an area can lead people to move to a different area. People might also move to an area where they perceive the political system to be better.
4. Cultural - People might move to another area where the population is more culturally similar to themselves or, in other cases, where it is different.

Tools and advancing technology

Even in the earliest stages of human development, humans have used tools to modify their environment. They killed animals for food, cleared out and even decorated caves for shelter, and gathered food from plants in the surrounding area. Although these tools were used to improve the human condition, as tools became more sophisticated they tended to lead to destruction of the environment. As tools advanced in technology, the ability of humans to modify their environment became even more powerful. The more complex technology becomes, the more potential it has to change the environment.

Anthropology

Anthropology studies human culture, both modern and prehistoric. Anthropology tells us about how ancient cultures lived, worked, and communicated; examines how different existing cultures function; analyzes languages and their use in individual and social contexts; and the behavior of our closest relatives, the primates, including chimpanzees and gorillas.

There are five major divisions in the field of anthropology:
1. Physical anthropology - Focuses on living humans and primates as well as fossil remains.
2. Primatology - Studies behavior of non-human primates.
3. Archaeology - Studies items and fossils left behind by prehistoric cultures and individuals.
4. Ethnography - Studies specific cultures by interacting with those cultures.
5. Linguistic anthropology - Studies various human languages.

Psychology

Psychology is the study of human behavior, especially as it applies to individuals and small groups. Psychologists try to determine reasons why people act the way they do, and help them to overcome specific problems.

The science of psychology is most often associated with the figures of Sigmund Freud and Karl Jung. In the education field, prominent psychologists include B. F. Skinner and Jean Piaget, who developed theories of learning. The three main types of psychologists are:
1. Cognitive psychologists - Focus on the process of thinking and learning and how it occurs
2. Clinical psychologists – Focus on abnormal behaviors
3. Social psychologists - Focus on behaviors of small groups of people

Assessment

As in other subjects, assessment in the social studies classroom involves three major goals:
1. Keep track of student progress to be sure they are meeting learning goals
2. Stay aware of specific needs of individual students and classrooms
3. Make changes to instruction or teaching methods if necessary to meet individual students' needs

Ideally, assessment should be performed both formally and informally to provide a more complete view of a student's understanding and progress. Formal assessment includes:
- Standardized tests
- Exams required at the district level
- Tests designed by the teacher

Informal assessment includes:
- Journals
- Portfolios
- Informal discussions
- Observation in the classroom

Arts, Music, and Physical Education

Maintaining an effective art classroom

Art exercises a variety of skills, including visual perception, design elements, and non-verbal expression. Art also allows students to exercise both fine motor skills and gross motor skills. To ensure students have the opportunity to properly develop art skills, an art classroom should include:
- Paper
- Pencils and pens
- Erasers
- Markers and crayons
- Paint and brushes
- Wrapping paper
- Newspapers and magazines
- Construction paper
- Scissors
- Glue
- Sculpting clay
- Beads
- Computers and graphics software

The types of materials that can contribute to a successful art program are limited only by the imagination of the teachers and the students. The wider the variety of materials available, the wider the variety of skills they will be able to explore.

Assessing student learning

Art instruction should include several basic goals to ensure appropriate learning and assessment:
- Giving students opportunities to experience, view and analyze a variety of art forms, styles and media
- Giving students opportunities to discuss reactions to art and their personal observations
- Teaching students about art styles and providing opportunities to discuss and identify various styles and movements
- Helping students learn to analyze art based on existing principles of art criticism as well as their personal reactions
- Teaching about aesthetics and aesthetic principles
- Teaching about art symbolism and other characteristics of works of art
- Giving students opportunities to create art in a variety of types and in many different media

Principles of design

In art classes, students must learn certain principles of design that will help them express themselves in artistic media. These principles are:
- Color - Includes primary, secondary, tertiary and compound colors, as well as the concepts of complementary and saturated colors
- Shape - Includes both positive and negative shapes
- Form - An entire structure, including its design and all its various elements
- Line - Where any two shapes meet, a line is formed; lines are often defined by pen, pencil or brush strokes
- Balance - Placing shapes, lines, color, etc., in a piece of art so that they complement each other
- Texture - Surface characteristics such as rough, smooth, or shiny; includes physical texture as well as visual texture
- Movement - Using artistic techniques to represent motion or action

Developing creative skills

All people respond to emotion, events or ideas through the use of art. To encourage children to develop and exercise these skills, it is important to present a variety of art materials, styles, techniques and media in the elementary classroom. This can include:
- Painting
- Drawing
- Crafts
- Sculpture
- Modeling
- Graphic arts
- Animation

Different students respond in different ways to different art techniques and forms. Providing a wide variety of options for artistic expression gives students the opportunity to determine which ones they like the best and feel most comfortable with. It also helps ensure that they do not fixate on a single technique, allowing them to widen their experience and means of expression.

Analyzing and critiquing art works

In the art classroom, students should learn vocabulary that is appropriate for critiquing and assessing art. This vocabulary should include the principles of design as well as the ability to answer analytical questions about the work's origin, function, cultural roots, purpose, and style. Students should also learn about various artistic styles, their historical importance, how they developed, and how to distinguish one artistic style from another. Students should also be taught to recognize the role of artwork in culture, such as whether art is created for a community or specific group, for commercial reasons, or simply as an expression of emotion or of the ideas of an individual artist.

Determining quality of work

In addition to knowing the appropriate vocabulary to discuss and analyze art, students should be able to employ these tools to determine the quality of an individual work of art. Criteria can include:
- Does the work use an appropriate style?
- Does the work succeed in its intended purpose?
- Is the work unique and memorable?
- Does the work represent a skilled use of the relevant techniques and media?

By asking these questions, students can move beyond simply identifying techniques, styles, and media and learn to make an informed judgment about the value of an individual work of art.

Music as an art form

Music seems to have begun as a means of expressing celebratory emotions or to accompany human rituals. Pairing music with words was probably a common early means to help remember cultural legends and other stories. The use of vocal arrangements and instrumental music follows specific rules regarding intervals and appropriate sound combinations. Musical notation records specific musical arrangements and instrumentations so that a piece of music can be duplicated.

Instrumental music began with simple instruments such as drums and flutes and has evolved into music that uses more complex instruments like the piano, harpsichord, guitar, or violin. Music is an important means of artistic communication that exists in every level of society.

Elements of music

Seven major elements work together to form a musical work:
1. Form - The structure of an individual work; includes elements of repetition and themes
2. Melody - The order in which notes are placed horizontally to form the main theme of a work.
3. Harmony - A vertical arrangement of notes that enhances the melody by being played simultaneously
4. Rhythm - Notes are held for varying amounts of time to produce the rhythm
5. Tone or timbre - The sound's quality; timbre can be mellow, strident, harsh, etc.

6. Texture - How various notes interact when they are produced simultaneously; this can include harmony as well as countermelodies
7. Dynamics - The varying volume of notes in the song; louder and softer dynamics add impact to the melody

Introducing instruments

Instrumental music offers students the ability to learn different types of musical expression, as well as the role of different types of instruments in other cultures. Students can learn basic instrumental skills that will be helpful if and when they decide to pursue an instrument in higher grades. Types of instruments usually used in elementary classrooms are one of three kinds:

- Rhythm instruments - Drums, sticks, triangles, blocks, tambourines and other simple percussion instruments are easy to play and introduce concepts of rhythm and playing instruments as a group.
- Melodic instruments - Bells or recorders are simple enough to play and help reinforce melodic concepts.
- Harmony instruments - The autoharp is a simple example of a harmony instrument, with which a child can easily produce chords to learn basic ideas of harmony.

Vocal music and singing techniques

When choosing vocal music for the classroom, teachers must consider its appropriateness not only in content but also in range. Children have a more limited vocal range than adults and should not be expected to sing beyond this range. In order to preserve vocal health and develop good singing habits, teachers should stress proper posture and breathing techniques in elementary music classes.

Teachers should also be sure the music used in the classroom represents a wide range of musical genres, styles, subjects and performance groups. Ensuring a wide variety of music helps students understand the cultural importance of music.

Reading music

Learning how to read musical notation early on will greatly enhance a student's ability to reproduce specific songs vocally or with a musical instrument. At this age level, teachers can begin with simple musical notation, using hash marks or other techniques to represent the length of individual notes and/or their relative pitches. Traditional music notation can follow, with students learning how to place notes on a musical staff. Some classes might discuss nontraditional music notation such as shape notes, where the shape of the note indicates its tonal value, or even Braille notation used for the blind.

Distinguishing types and styles of music

One of the best ways to help students learn to recognize different musical styles is through exposure. Styles introduced in the classroom could include:

- Jazz
- Classical
- Rock
- Latin
- Rhythm and blues (R&B)
- Country
- Folk

As students begin to recognize different styles of music, they will begin to understand how the different styles employ different rhythms, harmonies and other elements to produce their particular type of sound. Different types of music often evolve from different cultures and still other types from cultures combining musical approaches. Eventually, students will be able to identify not only musical styles and genres, but individual artists within specific genres.

Concepts and goals taught in music classes

Elementary level music curriculum focuses on several major goals:

- Teaching students how music is structured
- Teaching students how to listen to music in order to discern structure and other elements
- Exposing students to a variety of music styles and genres
- Encouraging students to make music and actively listen to it
- Helping students understand how music expresses emotion

In addition, students can begin to learn music vocabulary that can help them express their reactions to music and discuss musical form, structure and analysis in a way that others can easily understand. Providing the proper vocabulary for musical analysis can help students better understand music's cultural significance as well as its place in history and their own personal reactions to individual musical works.

Physical education

As our culture becomes more sedentary, physical education in school becomes more important. Students not only learn how to care for their bodies, but can learn ways to stay active and healthy throughout their lives. Physical activity helps build healthy bones and muscles and also prevents weight gain and the resulting health problems and therefore should be encouraged. The physical education curriculum also includes nutrition, health, and wellness, giving students knowledge that will help them pursue a healthy lifestyle. During physical education classes, teachers should be sure children are participating, but do not overexert. It is also important to be sure students are properly hydrated. Safety measures are important during physical education classes to prevent injury.

Health and wellness

Health and wellness topics can help students learn how to maintain their overall health in the long term. Some subjects included in the elementary health and wellness curriculum are:
- Weight control
- Importance of physical activity
- Common health issues
- Risk factors for common health issues, such as smoking or inappropriate diet
- Ways to avoid illness
- Overall hygiene
- Health care and what is available in different areas to different people
- Transmission of communicable diseases
- Diseases which are noncommunicable

Children can vastly improve their odds for long term good health by learning proper hygiene such as hand-washing, avoiding poor habits such as smoking, and by cultivating good habits such as exercise and proper diet.

Nutrition

In addition to reduced activity, poor eating habits contribute to poor health, childhood obesity, and long term health problems. In the elementary classroom, the study of nutrition helps students learn to make better food choices and to eat healthier and more balanced diets.

Major concepts in this subject at the elementary level include:
- Food Pyramid
- Major dietary building blocks such as proteins, fats and carbohydrates
- Vitamins and minerals and their roles in various aspects of overall health
- Types of carbohydrates; both simple and complex
- Types of fats; such as saturated and unsaturated
- Cholesterol, triglycerides, and their effects on health and well-being

Determining physical education curriculum

Although physical education is important at the elementary level, it is vital to be sure the instruction given is age-appropriate. Activities can be evaluated based on the three major domains of learning:
- Cognitive - Refers to thinking skills
- Psychomotor - Refers to physical skills and abilities
- Affective - Refers to emotional reactions or attitudes.

Children progress at different rates through these various domains of learning. Younger children might not have developed sufficient psychomotor skills for a rigorous sports activity, for instance, or might not have sufficient cognitive skills to understand the rules to a complicated game. Inappropriate levels of activities can lead to lack of engagement, hurt feelings, or even physical injuries. Teachers should always consider the needs and abilities of individuals as well as of the entire class when choosing physical education activities.

Planning a physical education activity

To ensure an activity will be safe and successful, the elementary teacher should consider the following factors:
- Assess the appropriateness of the environment where the activity will take place: Is the area safe? Is there sufficient room?
- Devise and put into practice routines that will keep students safe and help the activity go smoothly.
- Maintain a learning environment where children feel safe and supported in their efforts.
- Be sure both teachers and students know and are prepared to implement safety procedures if necessary.
- Establish rules and behavior guidelines. Teachers should let students help with this process—if they are invested in making the rules, they are more likely to follow them.
- Be sure any equipment or other resources are readily available.

Sports activities

Sports activities are often used in the physical education curriculum. This type of activity has several advantages and disadvantages.
Disadvantages include:
- Different skill levels can lead to students' feeling inferior or left out
- Intense competition can be emotionally difficult for younger students
- Students with physical differences or impairments can be subject to ridicule

Many of these disadvantages can be mitigated if teachers are careful to institute rules and procedures in the classroom that require students to demonstrate respect and support for each other.

Advantages include:

- Students learn to work together toward a goal
- Students experience competition in a controlled environment
- Students learn good sportsmanship

Motivating students to perform well in arts and physical education

Motivation is an important factor in a student's success. Teachers who can keep students motivated are likely to see better performance in their classrooms. Some strategies to increase motivation are:

- Take an interest in students and validate what they already know - Teachers can allow students to question them and show enthusiasm for the information that active learners bring to the classroom.
- Encourage mutual learning - Teachers can discuss their own thinking processes as they teach and allow students to share similar information to make learning a shared experience.
- Make learning relevant to the student - This includes providing interesting activities, using inclusive language, using collaborative learning techniques, and sharing stories in the classroom that help students relate better to both the teacher and the subject.

Practice Test

1. *Sea* and *see*, *fair* and *fare*, are called:
   a. Homophones
   b. Antonyms
   c. Homographs
   d. Twin words

2. In preparation for writing a paper, a high school class has been instructed to skim a number of Internet and print documents. They are being asked to:
   a. Read the documents several times, skimming to a deeper level of understanding each time
   b. Read the documents quickly, identifying those that offer the most specific information
   c. Read the documents quickly, looking for key words in order to gather the basic premise of each
   d. Read the documents carefully, looking for those that offer the most in-depth information

3. Which of the following is the best definition of Information Literacy?
   a. It is the set of skills required for reading and comprehending different information.
   b. It is the cognitive skill set necessary to amass a comprehensive base of knowledge.
   c. It is the skill set required for the finding, retrieval, analysis, and use of information.
   d. It is the set of skills necessary for effectively communicating information to others.

4. Which of the following choices describes the best introduction to a unit on oral traditions from around the world?
   a. Introducing games that practice new sight words, encoding words based on phonics rules, and answering short comprehension questions.
   b. Setting up video-conferencing with a school in Asia so that students can communicate with children from other countries.
   c. Inviting a guest speaker from a nearby Native American group to demonstrate oral story-telling to the class.
   d. Creating a PowerPoint presentation about various types of oral cultures and traditions and characteristics of each.

5. A syllable must contain:
    a. A vowel
    b. A consonant
    c. Both a vowel and a consonant
    d. A meaning

6. A ninth grade class is reading a 14-line poem in iambic pentameter. There are three stanzas of four lines each, and a two-line couplet at the end. Words at the end of each line rhyme with another word in the same stanza. The class is reading a:
    a. Sonnet
    b. Villanelle
    c. Sestina
    d. Limerick

7. According to MLA guidelines for writing research papers, which of the following is correct regarding citations of Web sources if you cannot immediately see the name of a source's author?
    a. Assume the author is not named, as this is a common occurrence on the Web.
    b. Do not name an agency or corporation as the author if it is the sponsor of the source.
    c. Author names are often on websites but need additional looking to discover.
    d. It is not permissible to cite the book or article title in lieu of an author's name.

8. A student says, "We learned that knowledge and understanding of language is important." This is an example of an error in which of these?
    a. Phonology
    b. Semantics
    c. Syntax
    d. Pragmatics

9. The purpose of corrective feedback is:
    a. To provide students with methods for explaining to the teacher or classmates what a passage was about
    b. To correct an error in reading a student has made, specifically clarifying where and how the error was made so that the student can avoid similar errors in the future
    c. To provide a mental framework that will help the student correctly organize new information
    d. To remind students that error is essential in order to truly understand and that it is not something to be ashamed of

10. A third grader knows he needs to write from left to right and from top to bottom on the page. He knows what sounds are associated with specific letters. He can recognize individual letters and can hear word families. He correctly identifies prefixes, suffixes, and homonyms, and his reading comprehension is very good. However, when he is asked to write, he becomes very upset. He has trouble holding a pencil, his letters are very primitively executed, and his written work is not legible. He most likely has:
   a. Dysgraphia
   b. Dyslexia
   c. Dyspraxia
   d. Nonverbal learning disorder

11. Which statement is correct regarding the relationship of your audience profile to the decisions you make in completing a writing assignment?
   a. How much time you spend on research is unrelated to your audience.
   b. Your audience does not influence how much information you include.
   c. The writing style, tone, and wording you use depend on your audience.
   d. How you organize information depends on structure, not on audience.

12. A classroom teacher observes that a new ELL student consistently omits the /h/ sound in words. Of these, what is the *first* factor the teacher should consider?
   a. The student may have an articulation disorder.
   b. The student may be a native Spanish speaker.
   c. The student may need a hearing assessment.
   d. The student may have a respiratory problem.

13. *Phone, they, church.* The underlined letters in these words are examples of:
   a. Consonant blend
   b. Consonant shift
   c. Continental shift
   d. Consonant digraph

14. Examples of onomatopoeia are:
   a. Sink, drink, mink, link
   b. Their, there, they're
   c. Drip, chirp, splash, giggle
   d. Think, in, thin, ink

15. Which of the following exercises would be the most appropriate tool for helping students evaluate the effectiveness of their own spoken messages?

a. Discuss written and oral assignments in class before completing them. Once the assignments are completed, the teacher meets individually with each student to discuss the content and effectiveness of each student's work.

b. Instruct students to present oral reports in class, which are then "graded" by classmates. A score of 1-10 is assigned based on students' perception of the reports' clarity. The student's average score determines his report's effectiveness.

c. Ask each student to prepare an oral report and a content quiz that highlights the report's main idea. The student then uses classmates' scores on the reviews to determine his report's effectiveness.

d. Put students into groups of three. Two students complete a role-playing assignment based on prompts provided by the teacher. The third student gives constructive feedback on how the other two can refine and clarify their speech.

16. When teaching students relationships between sounds and letters and between letters and words, what practices should teachers best follow?

a. Use a variety of instructional techniques, but including only the auditory and visual modes

b. Incorporate multisensory modalities within a variety of instructional strategies and materials

c. Always adhere to the same exact instructional method and materials to ensure consistency

d. Introduce similar-looking letters and similar-sounding phonemes together for discrimination

17. Which is greater, the number of English phonemes or the number of letters in the alphabet?

a. The number of letters in the alphabet, because they can be combined to create phonemes

b. The number of phonemes. A phoneme is the smallest measure of language sound

c. They are identical; each letter "owns" a correspondent sound

d. Neither. Phonemes and alphabet letters are completely unrelated

18. An understanding of the meanings of prefixes and suffixes such as *dis, mis, un, re, able,* and *ment* are important for:

a. Reading comprehension

b. Word recognition

c. Vocabulary building

d. Reading fluency

19. When considering strategies for writing assignments, it helps to know the cognitive (or learning) objective(s) your teacher is aiming to meet with an assignment. If the assignment asks you to "describe," "explain," "summarize," "restate," "classify," or "review" some material you read, what is the cognitive objective?
    a. Knowledge recall
    b. Application
    c. Comprehension
    d. Evaluation

20. Among the following, which is NOT a common academic standard for kindergarten students in decoding and identifying words?
    a. Showing knowledge that letter sequences correspond to phoneme sequences
    b. Understanding that word sounds and meanings change along with word letters
    c. Decoding monosyllabic words using initial and final consonant and vowel sounds
    d. Matching letters to consonant sounds; reading simple, monosyllabic sight words

21. Which of the following choices will be most important when designing a reading activity or lesson for students?
    a. Selecting a text
    b. Determining the number of students participating
    c. Analyzing the point in the school year at which the lesson is given
    d. Determining a purpose for instruction

22. Silent reading fluency can best be assessed by:
    a. Having the student retell or summarize the material to determine how much was understood
    b. Giving a written test that covers plot, theme, character development, sequence of events, rising action, climax, falling action, and outcome. A student must test at a 95% accuracy rate to be considered fluent at silent reading
    c. Giving a three-minute Test of Silent Contextual Reading Fluency four times a year. The student is presented with text in which spaces between words and all punctuation have been removed. The student must divide one word from another with slash marks, as in the following example: The/little/sailboat/bobbed/so/far/in/the/distance/it/looked/like/a/toy. The more words a student accurately separates, the higher her silent reading fluency score
    d. Silent reading fluency cannot be assessed. It is a private act between the reader and the text and does not invite critique

23. Which of the following strategies would not be helpful in building the word-identification skills of emergent readers?
    a. Allowing for invented spelling in written assignments or in-class work.
    b. Reinforcing phonemic awareness while reading aloud.
    c. Using dictionaries to look up unfamiliar words.
    d. Studying and reviewing commonly used sight words at the students' ability level.

24. According to English Language Arts and Reading, which of the following are students in grades 1-3 expected to do?
    a. Regularly read materials at the independent level, i.e., text containing one in 10 or fewer difficult words
    b. Select text to read independently using author knowledge, difficulty estimation, and personal interest
    c. Regularly read materials at the instructional level, i.e., text containing 1 in 20 or fewer difficult words
    d. Read aloud from unfamiliar texts fluently, i.e., with accuracy, phrasing, expression, and punctuation

25. A student is able to apply strategies to comprehend the meanings of unfamiliar words; can supply definitions for words with several meanings such as *crucial, criticism,* and *witness*; and is able to reflect on her background knowledge in order to decipher a word's meaning. These features of effective reading belong to which category?
    a. Word recognition
    b. Vocabulary
    c. Content
    d. Comprehension

26. Which of the following was the author of *The Pilgrim's Progress?*
    a. John Bunyan
    b. William Congreve
    c. Daniel Defoe
    d. Samuel Butler

27. Which of the following gives an example of a fallacy of inconsistency?
    a. "There are exceptions to all general statements."
    b. "Please pass me; my parents will be upset if I fail."
    c. "He is guilty: there is no evidence he is innocent."
    d. "Have you stopped cheating on your assignments?"

28. Which statement accurately reflects a principle regarding self-questioning techniques for increasing student reading comprehension?
    a. Asking only what kinds of "expert questions" fit the text's subject matter
    b. Asking only those questions that the text raises for the individual student
    c. Asking how each text portion relates to chapter main ideas is unnecessary
    d. Asking how the text information fits with what the student already knows

29. A student encounters a multisyllabic word. She's not sure if she's seen it before. What should she do first? What should she do next?
    a. Locate familiar word parts, then locate the consonants
    b. Locate the consonants, then locate the vowels
    c. Locate the vowels, then locate familiar word parts
    d. Look it up in the dictionary, then write down the meaning

30. In the model known in reading instruction as the Three Cueing Systems, which of these relate most to how sounds are used to communicate meaning?
    a. Syntactic cues
    b. Semantic cues
    c. Phonological cues
    d. Pragmatic cues

31. Which choice does not describe a common outcome of reading or writing?
    a. Communication of ideas
    b. Character development
    c. Enjoyment
    d. Language acquisition

32. Of the following examples, which one is *not* an open-ended question?
    a. "When does the climax of this story occur?"
    b. "Is this expression a simile or a metaphor?"
    c. "How are similes and metaphors different?"
    d. "What are some reasons we have poetry?"

33. *Bi, re,* and *un* are:
    a. Suffixes, appearing at the beginning of base words to change their meaning
    b. Suffixes, appearing at the end of base words to enhance their meaning
    c. Prefixes, appearing at the beginning of base words to emphasize their meaning
    d. Prefixes, appearing at the beginning of base words to change their meanings

34. Some experts maintain that teaching reading comprehension entails not just the application of skills, but the process of actively constructing meaning. This process they describe as *interactive, strategic,* and *adaptable*. Which of the following best defines the *interactive* aspect of this process?

a. The process involves the text, the reader, and the context in which reading occurs.
b. The process involves readers' using a variety of strategies in constructing meaning.
c. The process involves readers' changing their strategies to read different text types.
d. The process involves changing strategies according to different reasons for reading.

35. Mr. Harris divides his 3rd-grade English class into two sections each day. Approximately 60% of the class period is spent on phonics and sight word practice, and 40% is spent on learning comprehension strategies. Which statement is most true regarding Mr. Harris' approach?

a. This approach neglects several important components of language instruction.
b. This approach will bore the students and possibly create negative feelings about English class.
c. This approach will provide the best balance of reading instruction for this age group.
d. This approach could be improved by spending equal amounts of time on each component, as they are equally important.

36. After only two or three months into 1st grade, a new substitute teacher gives grades in the 80s to a student who had been receiving 100s from the regular teacher before the teacher had to take emergency leave. The substitute deducts points when the student occasionally reverses a letter or number, or misspells words like *biscuit, butterfly,* and *swallowed*. Which of the following most accurately describes this scenario?

a. The regular teacher should not have given 100s; the substitute grades errors more thoroughly.
b. The student should be evaluated for possible dyslexia because she reverses letters and numbers.
c. The student's writing is developmentally appropriate; the substitute's grading is inappropriate.
d. The student's occasional reversals are not important, but the misspellings need interventions.

37. Collaborative Strategic Reading (CSR) is a teaching technique that depends on two teaching practices. These practices are:

a. Cooperative learning and reading comprehension
b. Cooperative reading and metacognition
c. Reading comprehension and metacognition
d. Cooperative learning and metacognition

38. Which of the following is the most accurate characterization of dialects?
   a. They are non-standard versions of any language.
   b. They are often seen as less socially acceptable.
   c. They include linguistic features that are incorrect.
   d. They indicate poor/incomplete language learning.

39. Which of the following choices would be the least effective example of an integrated curriculum that includes language arts instruction?
   a. Ms. Smith, a language teacher, confers with Mr. Langston, a history and social studies teacher. Ms. Smith shows Mr. Langston how to model previewing and predicting skills before he introduces a new unit or assignment so that the students build their comprehension skills while reading for information.
   b. A science teacher recognizes that the students are having difficulty retaining information from their science textbooks when test time arrives. She creates a study guide with leading questions designed to help jog the students' memory about important concepts before the test.
   c. Ms. Shannon, an art teacher, plans a field trip to see the latest exhibit featuring a symbolic artist. A language teacher at her school joins the students at the museum to lead a discussion about the function of symbols and their meanings, as well as different methods of interpreting shared symbols in a society.
   d. A 1st-grade teacher uses children's books that introduce mathematical skills. For example, she reads a book weekly that tells a story about children preparing for a picnic, adding and subtracting items they need for the trip along the way. She encourages the children to solve the math questions along with her during the story.

40. A teacher has a student in her class who is not very motivated to write because he finds it difficult. She observes he has a highly visual learning style, does not like reading books but loves graphic novels, and has considerable artistic drawing talent and interest. Which of the following instructional strategies would best address his individual needs, strengths, and interests?
   a. Giving him audio recordings to accompany and guide his writing homework
   b. Letting him complete all assignments by drawing pictures instead of writing
   c. Having him draw the pictures and write accompanying text in graphic novels
   d. Providing and assigning him to view animated videos on the topic of writing

41. A reading teacher feels that some of his strategies aren't effective. He has asked a specialist to observe him and make suggestions as to how he can improve. The reading specialist should suggest that first:

    a. The teacher set up a video camera and record several sessions with different students for the specialist to review. The presence of an observer changes the outcome; if the specialist is in the room, it will negatively affect the students' ability to read

    b. The teacher reflects on his strategies himself. Which seem to work? Which don't? Can the teacher figure out why? It's always best to encourage teachers to find their own solutions so that they can handle future issues themselves

    c. They meet to discuss areas the teacher is most concerned about and decide on the teacher's goals

    d. The specialist should arrive unannounced to observe the teacher interacting with students. This will prevent the teacher from unconsciously over-preparing

42. Which of the following is an example of a portmanteau?

    a. Fax

    b. Brunch

    c. Babysitter

    d. Saxophone

43. Which answer choice describes the best sort of classroom modifications for a 1st-grade student with Auditory Processing Disorder?

    a. A multi-sensory literacy approach using tactile, kinesthetic, visual and auditory techniques in combination with systematic instruction.

    b. Modified lessons that teach concepts without the use of reading skills.

    c. Extra practice in reading on a daily basis.

    d. Creating engaging activities that will capture Amelia's interest in reading and introducing texts that will motivate her to complete lessons.

44. To measure children's emergent literacy development, an early childhood teacher informally evaluates their performance and behaviors during daily classroom activities. This is an example of what kind of assessment?

    a. Formative assessment

    b. Summative assessment

    c. Both (a) and (b)

    d. Neither (a) nor (b)

45. Round-robin reading refers to the practice of allowing children to take turns reading portions of a text aloud to the rest of the group during class. Which of the following statements is <u>least</u> true about this practice?

 a. Students have the chance to practice reading aloud with this strategy

 b. This practice is ineffective in its use of time, leaving students who are not reading aloud to become bored or daydream

 c. Round-robin reading lacks the creativity or engaging qualities that will interest students in building literacy skills

 d. This practice helps students feel comfortable with reading aloud due to continuous practice and encouragement from the teacher and peers

46. Which of the following correctly represents the sequence of stages or steps in the writing process?

 a. Prewriting, drafting, revising, editing, publishing

 b. Prewriting, drafting, editing, publishing, revising

 c. Prewriting, editing, drafting, revising, publishing

 d. Prewriting, drafting, editing, revising, publishing

47. The words chow, whoosh, and stalk all contain:

 a. Blends

 b. Digraphs

 c. Trigraphs

 d. Monoliths

48. Determine the number of diagonals of a dodecagon.

 a. 12

 b. 24

 c. 54

 d. 108

49. A dress is marked down by 20% and placed on a clearance rack, on which is posted a sign reading, "Take an extra 25% off already reduced merchandise." What fraction of the original price is the final sales price of the dress?

 a. $\dfrac{9}{20}$

 b. $\dfrac{11}{20}$

 c. $\dfrac{2}{5}$

 d. $\dfrac{3}{5}$

50. The graph below shows Aaron's distance from home at times throughout his morning run. Which of the following statements is (are) true?

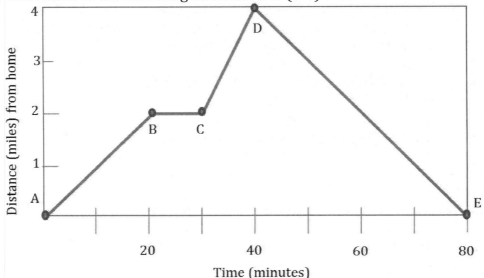

I.   Aaron's average running speed was 6 mph.
II. Aaron's running speed from point A to point B was the same as his running speed from point D to E.
III. Aaron ran a total distance of four miles.

   a. I only
   b. II only
   c. I and II
   d. I, II, and III

51. If a, b, and c are even integers and $3a^2 + 9b^3 = c$, which of these is the largest number which must be factor of c?

   a. 2
   b. 3
   c. 6
   d. 12

52. Solve $\frac{x-2}{x-1} = \frac{x-1}{x+1} + \frac{2}{x-1}$.

   a. $x = 2$
   b. $x = -5$
   c. $x = 1$
   d. No solution

- 76 -

53. Which of these is **NOT** a net of a cube?

a. b. c. d.

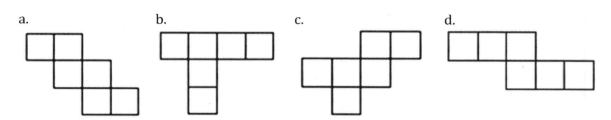

54. If the midpoint of a line segment graphed on the xy-coordinate plane is $(3, -1)$ and the slope of the line segment is -2, which of these is a possible endpoint of the line segment?
    a. $(-1, 1)$
    b. $(0, -5)$
    c. $(7, 1)$
    d. $(5, -5)$

55. A manufacturer wishes to produce a cylindrical can which can hold up to 0.5 L of liquid. To the nearest tenth, what is the radius of the can which requires the least amount of material to make?
    a. 2.8 cm
    b. 4.3 cm
    c. 5.0 cm
    d. 9.2 cm

56. Which of these does **NOT** simulate randomly selecting a student from a group of 11 students?
    a. Assigning each student a unique card value of A, 1, 2, 3, 4, 5, 6, 7, 8, 9, or J, removing queens and kings from a standard deck of 52 cards, shuffling the remaining cards, and drawing a single card from the deck
    b. Assigning each student a unique number 0-10 and using a computer to randomly generate a number within that range
    c. Assigning each student a unique number from 2 to 12; rolling two dice and finding the sum of the numbers on the dice
    d. All of these can be used as a simulation of the event.

57. Which of the following statements is true?
    a. A number is divisible by 6 if the number is divisible by both 2 and 3.
    b. A number is divisible by 4 if the sum of all digits is divisible by 8.
    c. A number is divisible by 3 if the last digit is divisible by 3.
    d. A number is divisible by 7 if the sum of the last two digits is divisible by 7.

58. A dress is marked down 45%. The cost, after taxes, is $39.95. If the tax rate is 8.75%, what was the original price of the dress?
   a. $45.74
   b. $58.61
   c. $66.79
   d. $72.31

59. Which of the following represents an inverse proportional relationship?
   a. $y = 3x$
   b. $y = \frac{1}{3}x$
   c. $y = \frac{3}{x}$
   d. $y = 3x^2$

60. What linear equation includes the data in the table below?

X	Y
−3	1
1	−11
3	−17
5	−23
9	−35

   a. y = −3x − 11
   b. y = −6x − 8
   c. y = −3x − 8
   d. y = −12x − 11

61. Tom needs to buy ink cartridges and printer paper. Each ink cartridge costs $30. Each ream of paper costs $5. He has $100 to spend. Which of the following inequalities may be used to find the combinations of ink cartridges and printer paper that he may purchase?
   a. $30c + 5p \leq 100$
   b. $30c + 5p < 100$
   c. $30c + 5p > 100$
   d. $30c + 5p \geq 100$

62. Eric has a beach ball with a radius of 9 inches. He is planning to wrap the ball with wrapping paper. Which of the following is the best estimate for the number of square feet of wrapping paper he will need?
   a. 4.08
   b. 5.12
   c. 7.07
   d. 8.14

63. Which of the following transformations has been applied to $\triangle ABC$?

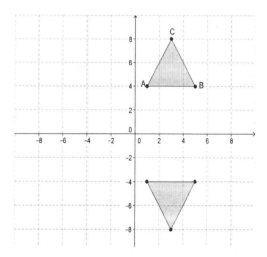

    a. translation
    b. rotation of 90 degrees
    c. reflection
    d. dilation

64. Kayla rolls a die and tosses a coin. What is the probability she gets an even number and heads?
    a. $\frac{1}{6}$
    b. $\frac{1}{4}$
    c. $\frac{1}{3}$
    d. 1

65. Mrs. Miller is teaching a unit on number and operations with her sixth grade class. At the beginning of class, she asks the students to work in groups to sketch a Venn diagram to classify whole numbers, integers, and rational numbers on a white board. Which of the following types of assessments has the teacher used?
    a. Summative assessment
    b. Formative assessment
    c. Formal assessment
    d. Informal assessment

66. Which of the following learning goals is most appropriate for a fourth grade unit on geometry and measurement?

    a. The students will be able to use a protractor to determine the approximate measures of angles in degrees to the nearest whole number.

    b. The students will be able to describe the process for graphing ordered pairs of numbers in the first quadrant of the coordinate plane.

    c. The students will be able to determine the volume of a rectangular prism with whole number side lengths in problems related to the number of layers times the number of unit cubes in the area of the base.

    d. The students will be able to classify two-dimensional figures in a hierarchy of sets and subsets using graphic organizers based on their attributes and properties.

67. Sophia is at the market buying fruit for her family of four. Kiwi fruit is only sold in packages of three. If Sophia would like each family member to have the same number of kiwi fruits, which of the following approaches can Sophia use to determine the fewest number of kiwi fruits she should buy?

    a. Sophia needs to determine the greatest common multiple of 3 and 4.

    b. Sophia needs to determine the least common multiple of 3 and 4.

    c. Sophia needs to determine the least common divisor of 3 and 4.

    d. Sophia needs to determine the greatest common divisor of 3 and 4.

68. A 6th grade math teacher is introducing the concept of positive and negative numbers to a group of students. Which of the following models would be the most effective when introducing this concept?

    a. Fraction strips

    b. Venn diagrams

    c. Shaded regions

    d. Number lines

69. Which of the following problems demonstrates the associative property of multiplication?

    a. $2(3 + 4) = 2(3) + 2(4)$

    b. $(3 \times 6) \times 2 = (4 \times 3) \times 3$

    c. $(2 \times 3) \times 4 = 2 \times (3 \times 4)$

    d. $6 \times 4 = 4 \times 6$

70. Which of the following is the correct solution for x in the system of equations $x - 1 = y$ and $y + 3 = 7$?

    a. $x = 6$

    b. $x = 5$

    c. $x = 4$

    d. $x = 8$

71. Which of the following best describes an isosceles triangle?
    a. A triangle with no sides of equal measurement and one obtuse angle
    b. A triangle with three sides of equal measurement
    c. A triangle with two sides of equal measurement and two acute angles
    d. A triangle with one right angle and two non-congruent acute angles

72. Mr. Amad draws a line with a slope of $-\frac{2}{3}$ on the white board through three points. Which of the sets could possibly be these three points?
    a. (-6, -2) (-7, -4), (-8, -6)
    b. (-4, 7), (-8, 13), (-6, 10)
    c. (-3, -1), (-6, 1), (0, -3)
    d. (-2, -3), (-1, -3), (0 -3)

73. Given this stem and leaf plot, what are the mean and median?

Stem	Leaf
1	6 8
2	0 1
3	4
4	5 9

    a. Mean = 28 and median = 20
    b. Mean = 29 and median = 20
    c. Mean = 29 and median = 21
    d. Mean = 28 and median = 21

74. The 6th grade teachers at Washington Elementary School are doing a collaborative unit on cherry trees. Miss Wilson's math classes are making histograms summarizing the heights of black cherry trees located at a local fruit orchard. How many of the trees at this local orchard are 73 feet tall?

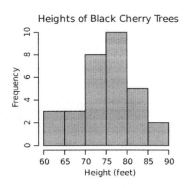

    a. 8
    b. That information cannot be obtained from this graph.
    c. 9
    d. 17

75. Elementary teachers in one school surveyed their students and discovered that 15% of their students have iPhones. Which of the following correctly states 15% in fraction, decimal, and ratio equivalents?

    a. $\frac{3}{20}$, 0.15, 3:20

    b. $\frac{3}{25}$, 0.15, 3:25

    c. $\frac{15}{10}$, 1.5%, 15:10

    d. $\frac{2}{1}$, 1.5%, 2:1

76. Mrs. Vories, a fifth grade teacher, asks her class to use compatible numbers to help her determine approximately how many chicken nuggets she needs to buy for a school-wide party. The school has 589 students and each student will be served nine nuggets. Which student correctly applied the concept of compatible numbers?

    a. Madison estimates: $500 \times 10 = 5,000$ nuggets

    b. Audrey estimates: $600 \times 5 = 3,000$ nuggets

    c. Ian estimates: $600 \times 10 = 6,000$ nuggets

    d. Andrew estimates: $500 \times 5 = 2,500$ nuggets

77. The table below shows the average amount of rainfall Houston receives during the summer and autumn months.

Month	Amount of Rainfall (in inches)
June	5.35
July	3.18
August	3.83
September	4.33
October	4.5
November	4.19

What percentage of rainfall received during this timeframe, is received during the month of October?

    a. 13.5%

    b. 15.1%

    c. 16.9%

    d. 17.7%

78. A can has a radius of 1.5 inches and a height of 3 inches. Which of the following best represents the volume of the can?

    a. 17.2 in^3

    b. 19.4 in^3

    c. 21.2 in^3

    d. 23.4 in^3

79. What is the area of the shaded region in the figure shown below?

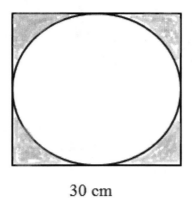

30 cm

30 cm

    a. 177 cm²
    b. 181 cm²
    c. 187 cm²
    d. 193 cm²

80. What is the perimeter of the trapezoid graphed below?

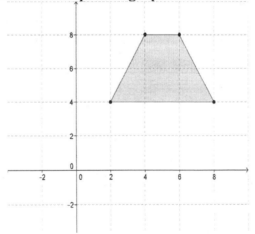

    a. $4 + \sqrt{10}$
    b. $8 + 4\sqrt{5}$
    c. $4 + 2\sqrt{5}$
    d. $8 + 2\sqrt{22}$

81. What is the slope of the leg marked x in the triangle graphed below?

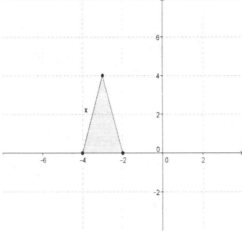

    a. 2
    b. 3.5
    c. 4
    d. 4.5

82. $A = \{5, 9, 2, 3, -1, 8\}$ and $B = \{2, 0, 4, 5, 6, 8\}$. What is $A \cap B$?
    a. $\{5, 2, 8\}$
    b. $\{-1, 0, 2, 3, 4, 5, 6, 8, 9\}$
    c. $\emptyset$
    d. $\{5, 8\}$

83. In a pack of 20 jelly beans, there are two licorice- and four cinnamon-flavored jelly beans. What is the probability of choosing a licorice jelly bean followed by a cinnamon jelly bean?

    a. $\dfrac{2}{5}$

    b. $\dfrac{8}{20}$

    c. $\dfrac{2}{95}$

    d. $\dfrac{1}{50}$

84. Amy saves $450 every 3 months. How much does she save after 3 years?
    a. $4,800
    b. $5,200
    c. $5,400
    d. $5,800

85. Which of the following statements is *not* true regarding English expansionism in the 16th century?
    a. England's defeat of the Spanish Armada in 1588 brought a decisive end to their war with Spain.
    b. King Henry VIII's desire to divorce Catherine of Aragon strengthened English expansionism.
    c. Queen Elizabeth's support for the Protestant Reformation strengthened English expansionism.
    d. Sir Francis Drake and other English sea captains plundered the Spaniards' plunders of Indians.

86. During the decolonization of the Cold War years, which of the following events occurred chronologically latest?
    a. The Eastern Bloc and Satellite states became independent from the Soviet Union
    b. Canada became totally independent from British Parliament via the Canada Act
    c. The Bahamas, in the Caribbean, became independent from the United Kingdom
    d. The Algerian War ended, and Algeria became independent from France

87. Who negotiates treaties?
    a. The President
    b. The House of Representatives
    c. Ambassadors
    d. The Senate

88. How long can members of the Federal Judiciary serve?
    a. Four years
    b. Eight years
    c. For life
    d. Six years

89. Guaranteed rights enumerated in the *Declaration of Independence*, possessed by all people, are referred to as:
    a. Universal rights
    b. Unalienable rights
    c. Voting rights
    d. Peoples' rights

90. Which of the following statements is *not* true about the Gilded Age in America?
    a. The Gilded Age was the era of the "robber barons" in the business world
    b. The Gilded Age got its name from the excesses of the wealthy upper-class
    c. The Gilded Age had philanthropy Carnegie called the "Gospel of Wealth"
    d. The Gilded Age is a term whose origins have not been identified clearly

91. Which of the following exemplifies the multiplier effect of large cities?
    a. The presence of specialized equipment for an industry attracts even more business.
    b. The large population lowers the price of goods.
    c. Public transportation means more people can commute to work.
    d. A local newspaper can afford to give away the Sunday edition.

92. Criminal cases are tried under:
    I.   State law
    II.   Federal law
    III.   Civil court
    a. I and III
    b. II only
    c. I only
    d. I and II

93. Which of the following is *not* a true statement regarding the Louisiana Purchase?
    a. Jefferson sent a delegation to Paris to endeavor to purchase only the city of New Orleans from Napoleon.
    b. Napoleon, anticipating U.S. intrusions into Louisiana, offered to sell the U.S. the entire Louisiana territory.
    c. The American delegation accepted Napoleon's offer, though they were only authorized to buy New Orleans.
    d. The Louisiana Purchase, once it was completed, increased the territory of the U.S. by 10% overnight.

94. The idea that the purpose of the American colonies was to provide Great Britain with raw materials and a market for its goods is an expression of:
    a. Free trade.
    b. Most favored nation status.
    c. Mercantilism.
    d. Laissez-faire capitalism.

95. During the early Medieval period in Europe, before the 5th century, where were the main centers of literacy found?
    a. They were in the homes of the wealthy
    b. They were in the churches and monasteries
    c. They were in the local artisan and craft guilds
    d. There were no centers of literacy

96. How must inferior courts interpret the law?
    a. According to the Supreme Court's interpretation
    b. According to the Constitution
    c. However they choose
    d. According to the political climate

97. Which entity in American government is the closest to true democracy?
  a. The Electoral College
  b. The House of Representatives
  c. Committees within the Senate
  d. The Supreme Court

98. Power divided between local and central branches of government is a definition of what term?
  a. Bicameralism
  b. Checks and balances
  c. Legislative oversight
  d. Federalism

99. Virginian _____ advocated a stronger central government and was influential at the Constitutional Convention.
  a. Benjamin Franklin
  b. James Madison
  c. George Mason
  d. Robert Yates

100. Which of the following will result if two nations use the theory of comparative advantage when making decisions of which goods to produce and trade?
  a. Each nation will make all of their own goods
  b. Both nations will specialize in the production of the same specific goods
  c. Each nation will specialize in the production of different specific goods
  d. Neither nation will trade with one another

101. The Presidential veto of legislation passed by Congress illustrates which principal in American government?
  a. Checks and balances
  b. Federal regulation
  c. Freedom of speech
  d. Separation of church and state

102. A filibuster is used to delay a bill. Where can a filibuster take place?
  I.   The House
  II.   The Senate
  III. Committees
  a. I only
  b. II only
  c. I and II
  d. I, II, and III

103. To be President of the United States, one must meet these three requirements:
   a. The President must be college educated, at least 30 years old, and a natural citizen
   b. The President must be a natural citizen, have lived in the U.S. for 14 years, and have a college education
   c. The President must be a natural citizen, be at least 35 years old, and have lived in the U.S. for 14 years
   d. The President must be at least 30 years old, be a natural citizen, and have lived in the U.S. for 14 years

104. Which of the following is most likely to benefit from inflation?
   a. A bond investor who owns fixed-rate bonds
   b. A retired widow with no income other than fixed Social Security payments
   c. A person who has taken out a fixed-rate loan
   d. A local bank who has loaned money out at fixed rate

105. After the Civil War, urban populations increased. This growth was likely due to:
   a. An increased reliance on agriculture
   b. The Industrial Revolution
   c. Prohibition
   d. Slavery persisting in some areas

106. As a form of government, what does oligarchy mean?
   a. Rule by one
   b. Rule by a few
   c. Rule by law
   d. Rule by many

107. The Trail of Tears was:
   a. The forced removal of British soldiers after the American Revolution
   b. The forced evacuation of Cherokee peoples into Oklahoma
   c. The forced evacuation of freed slaves from the South after the Civil War
   d. The tears of Betsy Ross while she sewed the first American flag

108. What is the main reason that tropical regions near the Equator tend to experience relatively constant year-round temperatures?
   a. They are usually located near the ocean
   b. The angle at which sunlight hits them remains relatively constant throughout the year
   c. They are located along the "Ring of Fire"
   d. They do not have seasons

109. Which of the following is *not* correct regarding assumptions of mercantilism?
    a. The money and the wealth of a nation are identical properties
    b. In order to prosper, a nation should try to increase its imports
    c. In order to prosper, a nation should try to increase its exports
    d. Economic protectionism by national governments is advisable

110. Which scientist first proposed the heliocentric universe instead of a geocentric one?
    a. Galileo
    b. Ptolemy
    c. Copernicus
    d. Isaac Newton

111. Congressional elections are held every _____ years.
    a. Four
    b. Two
    c. Six
    d. Three

112. All else being equal, which of the following locations is likely to have the coolest climate?
    a. A city located at 6,000 feet above sea level
    b. A city located at 500 feet above sea level
    c. A city that receives less than 10 inches of precipitation per year
    d. A city that receives more than 50 inches of precipitation per year

113. Which Italian Renaissance figure was best known as a political philosopher?
    a. Dante Alighieri
    b. Leonardo Da Vinci
    c. Francesco Petrarca
    d. Niccolò Machiavelli

114. Scientists often form hypotheses based on particular observations. Which of the following is NOT true of a good hypothesis?
    a. A good hypothesis is complex.
    b. A good hypothesis is testable.
    c. A good hypothesis is logical.
    d. A good hypothesis predicts future events.

115. What will happen to light waves as they hit a convex lens?
    a. They will be refracted and converge.
    b. They will be refracted and diverge.
    c. They will be reflected and converge.
    d. They will be reflected and diverge.

116. Which of the following animal structures is not paired to its correct function?
    a. Muscle System – controls movement through three types of muscle tissue
    b. Nervous System – controls sensory responses by carrying impulses away from and toward the cell body
    c. Digestive System – breaks down food for absorption into the blood stream where it is delivered to cells for respiration
    d. Circulatory System – exchanges gasses with the environment by delivering oxygen to the bloodstream and releasing carbon dioxide

117. What change occurs when energy is added to a liquid?
    a. a phase change
    b. a chemical change
    c. sublimation
    d. condensation

118. After a science laboratory exercise, some solutions remain unused and are left over. What should be done with these solutions?
    a. Dispose of the solutions according to local disposal procedures.
    b. Empty the solutions into the sink and rinse with warm water and soap.
    c. Ensure the solutions are secured in closed containers and throw away.
    d. Store the solutions in a secured, dry place for later use.

119. If an atom has a neutral charge, what must be true of the atom?
    a. The nucleus contains only neutrons and no protons.
    b. The atomic mass is equal to the number of neutrons.
    c. The atomic number is equal to the number of neutrons.
    d. The atomic number is equal to the number of electrons.

120. Which of the following words is not connected to the process of mountain building?
    a. Folding
    b. Faulting
    c. Transform
    d. Convergent

121. What laboratory practice can increase the accuracy of a measurement?
    a. repeating the measurement several times
    b. calibrating the equipment each time you use it
    c. using metric measuring devices
    d. following SDS information

122. Elements on the periodic table are arranged into groups and periods and ordered according to all of the following except
    a. atomic number.
    b. refractive index
    c. reactivity.
    d. number of protons.

123. A gas is held in a closed container and held at constant temperature. What is the effect of increasing the volume of the container by 3 times?
    a. The pressure is tripled.
    b. The pressure increases by one-third.
    c. The pressure decreases by one-third.
    d. The pressure remains constant.

124. Which of the following terms describes an intrusion of magma injected between two layers of sedimentary rock, forcing the overlying strata upward to create a dome-like form?
    a. Sill
    b. Dike
    c. Laccolith
    d. Caldera

125. Which of the following is needed for an experiment to be considered successful?
    a. a reasonable hypothesis
    b. a well-written lab report
    c. data that others can reproduce
    d. computer-aided statistical analysis

126. Which of the following statements about heat transfer is not true?
    a. As the energy of a system changes, its thermal energy must change or work must be done.
    b. Heat transfer from a warmer object to a cooler object can occur spontaneously.
    c. Heat transfer can never occur from a cooler object to a warmer object.
    d. If two objects reach the same temperature, energy is no longer available for work.

127. A man accidentally drops his wallet in a swimming pool. He can see his wallet at the bottom of the pool. He jumps in to retrieve it, but the wallet is not where it appeared to be. What is the reason for the optical illusion?
    a. The reflection of sunlight off of the water disrupted his view
    b. Light is refracted as it exits the water, changing the wallet's apparent location
    c. The current at the bottom of the pool caused the wallet to move
    d. The heat from the Sun has impaired the man's vision

128. The precision of a number of data points refers to:
    a. How accurate the data is
    b. How many errors the data contains
    c. How close the data points are to the mean of the data
    d. How close the actual data is to the predicted result

129. The most recently formed parts of the Earth's crust can be found at:
    a. Subduction zones.
    b. Compressional boundaries.
    c. Extensional boundaries.
    d. Mid-ocean ridges.

130. Which type of nuclear process features atomic nuclei splitting apart to form smaller nuclei?
    a. Fission
    b. Fusion
    c. Decay
    d. Ionization

131. How does adding a solute to a liquid solvent affect the vapor pressure of the liquid?
    a. The vapor pressure increases by an amount proportional to the amount of solute.
    b. The vapor pressure increases by an amount proportional to the amount of solvent.
    c. The vapor pressure decreases by an amount proportional to the amount of solute.
    d. The amount of solute present in a liquid solvent does not have any effect on vapor pressure.

132. What drives weather systems to move west to east in the mid-latitudes?
    a. The prevailing westerlies
    b. The prevailing easterlies
    c. The trade winds
    d. The doldrums

133. How are organisms, such as snakes, cacti, and coyotes, able to survive in harsh desert conditions?
    a. Over thousands of years, these organisms have developed adaptations to survive in arid climates
    b. These organisms migrate out of the desert during the summer months, only living in the desert for a portion of the year
    c. Snakes, cacti, and coyotes work together to find sources of food and water
    d. Snakes, cacti, and coyotes are all aquatic species that live in ponds and rivers during the hot day

134. In which of the following scenarios is work not applied to the object?
    a. Mario moves a book from the floor to the top shelf.
    b. A book drops off the shelf and falls to the floor.
    c. Mario pushes a box of books across the room.
    d. Mario balances a book on his head.

135. Which of the following would not be used as evidence for evolution?
    a. Fossil record
    b. DNA sequences
    c. Anatomical structures
    d. Reproductive habits

136. Which of the following is considered a non-renewable resource?
    a. Glass
    b. Wood
    c. Cattle
    d. Soil

137. The stream of charged particles that escape the Sun's gravitational pull is best described by which of the following terms?
    a. Solar wind
    b. Solar flare
    c. Solar radiation
    d. Sunspots

138. According to Ohm's Law, how are voltage and current related in an electrical circuit?
    a. Voltage and current are inversely proportional to one another.
    b. Voltage and current are directly proportional to one another.
    c. Voltage acts to oppose the current along an electrical circuit.
    d. Voltage acts to decrease the current along an electrical circuit.

139. Where are the reproductive organs of a plant?
    a. Style
    b. Stigma
    c. Flowers
    d. Sepals

140. What is the definition of work?
    a. the amount of energy used to accomplish a job
    b. the force used to move a mass over a distance
    c. the amount of energy used per unit of time
    d. energy stored in an object due to its position

141. Which of the following organelles is/are formed when the plasma membrane surrounds a particle outside of the cell?
    a. Golgi bodies
    b. Rough endoplasmic reticulum
    c. Secretory vesicles
    d. Endocytic vesicles

142. Which of the following is not one of the primary elements of art?
    a. Dimension
    b. Unity
    c. Texture
    d. Space

143. Drybrush is a technique that is primarily used in
    a. watercolor painting.
    b. oil painting.
    c. acrylic painting.
    d. ceramic glazing.

144. An art teacher wants to incorporate the subjects students are learning in their general education classes into his art lesson. Which of the following lessons could be best incorporated into his art class?
    a. A social studies lesson on political propaganda
    b. A math lesson on equations
    c. An English lesson about haiku
    d. A science lesson about metabolic efficiency

145. Diminished chords are considered dissonant for which of the following reasons:
    a. They sound "sad."
    b. They lack a tonal center.
    c. They are barely audible.
    d. They are viewed with universal disdain and absent from most popular recordings.

146. Which of the following terms refers to the relative lightness or darkness of color in a painting?
    a. Hue
    b. Intensity
    c. Value
    d. Texture

147. Which of the following artistic elements is most commonly used to create the illusion of depth in a painting?
    a. Balance
    b. Line
    c. Contrast
    d. Symmetry

148. Which of these locomotor activities is most appropriate for children younger than five years old?
    a. Blob tag
    b. Musical hoops
    c. Follow the leader
    d. Any of these equally

149. Of the four types of diseases—cancers, cardiovascular diseases, diabetes, and respiratory diseases—that cause the majority of deaths from noncommunicable diseases, which risk factor is not common to all four types?
    a. Unsafe water
    b. Drinking alcohol
    c. Poor diet
    d. Smoking tobacco

150. The advantage of drawing with charcoal as opposed to lead pencils is that
    a. charcoal can be smudged to create shading.
    b. charcoal does not require a fixative.
    c. charcoal is available in a variety of hues.
    d. charcoal is available in a wide range of different values, ranging from dark and soft to light and hard.

Answers and Explanations

1. A: Homophones. Homophones are a type of homonym that sound alike but are spelled differently and have different meanings. Other examples are *two, to,* and *too; their, they're,* and *there.*

2. C: Read the documents quickly, looking for key words in order to gather the basic premise of each. Skimming allows a reader to quickly gain a broad understanding of a piece of writing in order to determine if a more thorough reading is warranted. Skimming allows students who are researching a topic on the Internet or in print to consider a substantial body of information in order to select only that of particular relevance.

3. C: According to the Association of College and Research Libraries, Information Literacy is the set of skills that an individual must have for finding, retrieving, analyzing, and using information. It is required not just for reading and understanding information (A). Information Literacy does not mean learning and retaining a lot of information (B), or only sharing it with others (D), but rather knowing how to find information one does not already have and how to evaluate that information critically for its quality and apply it judiciously to meet one's purposes.

4. C: Oral language is a vital aspect of any language arts instruction. Often, the first concepts of language are transmitted via oral and auditory processes. The first Americans also possessed a rich oral culture in which stories and histories were passed down through generations via storytelling. Inviting a guest speaker who is part of this culture helps students understand more about cultures in their world, as well as the value of oral language and storytelling. This introduction gives students a relevant personal experience with which to connect what they will be learning in class.

5. A: A vowel. A syllable is a minimal sound unit arranged around a vowel. For example, *academic* has four syllables: *a/ca/dem/ic.* It is possible for a syllable to be a single vowel, as in the above example. It is not possible for a syllable to be a single consonant.

6. A: Sonnet. There are three primary types of sonnets. The Shakespearean sonnet is specifically what these students are reading. A Spenserian sonnet is also composed of three four-line stanzas followed by a two-line couplet; however, the rhymes are not contained within each stanza but spill from one stanza to the next (*abab bcbc cdcd ee*). A Petrarchan sonnet divides into an eight-line stanza and a six-line stanza.

7. C: On the Internet, it often occurs that the name of the author of an article or book is actually provided but is not obviously visible at first glance. Web sources

- 96 -

frequently include the author's name, but on another page of the same site, such as the website's home page; or in a tiny font at the very end of the web page, rather than in a more conspicuous location. In such cases, students doing online research may have to search more thoroughly than usual to find the author's name. Therefore, they should not immediately assume the author is not named (A). Also, many Web sources are sponsored by government agencies or private corporations and do not give individual author names. In these cases, the research paper *should* cite the agency or corporation name as author (B). Finally, it is much more common for online sources to omit an author's name than it is in print sources. In these cases, it is both permitted and advised by the MLA to cite the article or book title instead (D).

8. C: The example has an error in subject-verb agreement, which is a component of syntax (sentence structure and word order). Phonology (A) involves recognition and production of speech sounds and phonemes, including differentiation, segmentation, and blending. Semantics (B) involves the meanings of words. Pragmatics (D) involves the social use of language to communicate and meet one's needs.

9. B: To correct an error in reading a student has made, specifically clarifying where and how the error was made so that the student can avoid similar errors in the future. A reading teacher offers corrective feedback to a student in order to explain why a particular error in reading is, in fact, an error. Corrective feedback is specific; it locates where and how the student went astray so that similar errors can be avoided in future reading.

10. A: Dysgraphia. Dysgraphic individuals have difficulty with the physical act of writing. They find holding and manipulating a pencil problematic. Their letters are primitively formed, and their handwriting is illegible.

11. C: The kind of audience for whom you are writing, as well as your purpose for writing, will determine what style, tone, and wording you choose. Knowing who your audience is will enable you to select writing strategies, a style and tone, and specific word choices that will be most understandable and appealing to your readers. Knowing the type of audience will also dictate how much time to spend on research (A). Some readers will expect more supporting evidence while others will be bored or overwhelmed by it. Similarly, you will want to include more or less information depending on who will be reading what you write (B). And while the structure of your piece does inform how you organize your information, you should also vary your organization according to who will read it (D).

12. B: In the Spanish language, the letter *h* is typically silent. Because the student is an ELL and the USA has many people—both immigrants and those born here—whose first and/or only language is Spanish, this is the first factor to consider among the choices. An articulation disorder (A) is possible, but the teacher should not assume this first with an ELL student. (An SLP evaluation can determine the

difference.) While hearing assessment (C) is always a good idea, if /h/ omission were due to hearing loss the student would likely omit or distort other unvoiced fricatives like /f/, /s/, /ʃ/, and /θ/. If the student had a breathing problem (D), other symptoms would occur in addition to not articulating /h/.

13. D: Consonant digraph. A consonant digraph is a group of consonants in which all letters represent a single sound.

14. C: *Drip, chirp, splash, giggle.* Onomatopoeia refers to words that sound like what they represent.

15. C: Each answer can be an effective tool in teaching students to build oral language skills. The question makes clear that the objective is to help students evaluate their own oral language skills, which will assist them in both spoken and written assignments. The only answer choice that involves the student himself evaluating his message is choice C. When the student prepares a review/quiz based upon important information, he or she will be more able to speak specifically to that information. When classmates complete the review, the student can identify any patterns in the questions' answers that give clues as to how well those main ideas were communicated. In this way, the student can evaluate how effective the oral presentation was, without relying on classmates or the teacher.

16. B: Teachers should apply a variety of instructional techniques to enable students with different strengths, needs, and learning styles to understand sound-letter and letter-word relationships, but they should not restrict the instructional modalities to auditory and visual (A) simply because sounds are auditory and letters are visual. Multisensory modalities (B) are more effective because different students use different senses to learn; redundancy is necessary for learning; and input to multiple senses affords a more multidimensional learning experience, promoting comprehension and retention. While some aspects of this instruction should be consistent (e.g., starting with high-frequency letters and with phonemes children can produce more easily), sticking to only one method and set of materials (C) prevents using variety to reach all students. Visually similar letters and auditorily similar phonemes should *not* be introduced together (D) before students can discriminate among them; teachers should begin with more obvious differences.

17. B: The number of phonemes. A phoneme is the smallest measure of language sound. English-language phonemes, about 40 in number, are composed of individual letters as well as letter combinations. A number of letters have more than one associated sound. For example, "c" can be pronounced as a hard "c" (cake) or a soft "c" (Cynthia). Vowels, in particular, have a number of possible pronunciations.

18. A: Reading comprehension. Prefixes and suffixes change the meanings of the root word to which they are attached. A student who understands that *un* means

"not" will be able to decipher the meanings of words such as *unwanted, unhappy,* or *unreasonable.*

19. C: The verbs quoted all refer to interpreting information in your own words. This task targets the cognitive objective of comprehension. Tasks targeting the cognitive objective of knowledge recall (A) would ask you to name, label, list, define, repeat, memorize, order, or arrange the information. Tasks targeting the cognitive objective of application (B) would ask you to calculate, solve, practice, operate, sketch, use, prepare, illustrate, or apply the material. Tasks targeting the cognitive objective of evaluation (D) would ask you to judge, appraise, evaluate, conclude, predict, score, or compare the information.

20. C: Decoding monosyllabic words by referring to the initial and final consonant, short vowel, and long vowel sounds represented by their letters is a common academic standard for 1st-grade students. Typical academic standards for kindergarten students include demonstrating knowledge of letter-sound correspondences (A); understanding the alphabetic principle (B); matching letters to their corresponding consonant (and short vowel) sounds; and reading simple, monosyllabic sight words (D), i.e., high-frequency words.

21. D: It is impossible to include every text desired into the language curriculum—there are simply too many good books, stories, poems, speeches, and media available. Teachers must first think about what skills their students need to acquire, as well as what skills they have already mastered. In designing activities for class, a good teacher will start first with the purpose for instruction (or perceiving oral or visual text such as video or music). For example, purposes of reading can include: reading for information; reading for enjoyment; understanding a message; identifying main or supporting ideas; or developing an appreciation for artistic expression/perception. Once the purpose or intended learning outcome has been identified, the teacher will have a much better idea of which texts, strategies, and activities will support that purpose.

22. C: Giving a three-minute Test of Silent Contextual Reading Fluency four times a year. The student is presented with text in which spaces between words and all punctuation have been removed. The student must divide one word from another with slash marks, as in the following example: *The/little/sailboat/bobbed/so/far/in/the/distance/it/looked/like/a/toy.* The more words a student accurately separates, then the higher her silent reading fluency score. Silent reading fluency can be monitored over time by giving the Test of Silent Contextual Reading Fluency (TSCRF) four times a year. A similar assessment tool is the Test of Silent Word Reading Fluency (TOSWRF), in which words of increasing complexity are given as a single, undifferentiated, and unpunctuated strand. As with the TSCRF, three minutes are given for the student to separate each word from the next. *Itwillcannotschoolbecomeagendaconsistentphilosophysuperfluous* is an example of such a strand.

23. A: Emergent readers are those who are not yet reading fluently (with appropriate speed and accuracy). Choice B refers to the practice of reviewing relationships between letters and sounds, which is vital to building reading skills. Choice C would help students build vocabulary retention by requiring them to find unfamiliar words in the dictionary. This practice causes the student to analyze and retain spelling of unfamiliar words, as well as reinforces dictionary/reference skills. Choice D addresses the fact that many words in the English language are irregularly spelled and cannot be decoded with conventional phonetic instruction. While invented spelling described in Choice A may be permitted in emergent readers, this practice is not likely to build specific reading skills.

24. B: Standards expect 1st- to 3rd-graders to read materials regularly that are at the independent level, which they define as text where approximately one in 20 words or fewer are difficult for the student—not one in 10 (A). Students are also expected to select text to read independently, informed by their knowledge of authors, text genres and types; their estimation of text difficulty levels; and their personal interest (B). They should also read text regularly that is at the instructional level, which they define as including no more than one in 10 words the reader finds difficult—not one in 20 (C). Finally, standards expect students to read aloud fluently from familiar texts, not unfamiliar ones (D).

25. B: Vocabulary. Strategizing in order to understand the meaning of a word, knowing multiple meanings of a single word, and applying background knowledge to glean a word's meaning are all ways in which an effective reader enhances vocabulary. Other skills include an awareness of word parts and word origins, the ability to apply word meanings in a variety of content areas, and a delight in learning the meanings of unfamiliar words.

26. A: John Bunyan (1628-1688) was the author of *The Pilgrim's Progress*, a religious allegory, among many other works. William Congreve (B) (1670-1729) wrote *The Way of the World*, originally a play not successful on the theater stage, but subsequently highly regarded as a literary exemplar of the comedy of manners. Daniel Defoe (C) (circa 1660-1731) is known for *Robinson Crusoe* and other adventure novels, and *The Apparition of Mrs. Veal*, a ghost story later found to be factually based. Samuel Butler (D) (1612-1680), one of the Augustan poets, wrote the burlesque poem *Hudibras*.

27. A: A fallacy of inconsistency exists in a statement that contradicts itself or defeats itself. Saying there are exceptions to all general statements is itself a general statement; therefore, according to the content, this statement must also have an exception, implying there are NOT exceptions to all general statements. Option B is an example of a fallacy of irrelevance: passing or failing is determined by course performance, so asking to pass because parents will be upset if one fails is an irrelevant reason for appealing to a teacher for a passing grade. Choice C is an example of a fallacy of insufficiency: a statement is made with insufficient evidence to support it. A lack of evidence of innocence is not enough to prove one is guilty

because there could also be an equal lack of evidence of guilt. Option D is an example of a fallacy of inappropriate presumption: asking someone if s/he has stopped cheating presumes that s/he has cheated in the past. The person being asked this question cannot answer either "yes" or "no" without confirming that s/he has indeed been cheating. If the person being asked has not been cheating, then the person asking the question is making a false assumption.

28. D: When students ask themselves how the information in a text they are reading fits with what they already know, they are relating the text to their own prior knowledge, which increases their reading comprehension. Students should not only ask themselves what kinds of "expert questions" fit the subject matter of the text (A)—e.g., classification, physical, and chemical properties are typical question topics in science; genre, character, plot, and theme are typical of literature questions; sequence, cause-and-effect, and comparison-contrast questions are typical of history—but also what questions the material brings up for them personally (B). It is necessary and important for students to ask themselves continually how each text portion relates to its chapter's main ideas (C) as they read to optimize their reading comprehension and retention.

29. C: Locate the vowels, then locate familiar word parts. Syllables are organized around vowels. In order to determine the syllables, this student should begin by locating the vowels. It's possible to have a syllable that is a single vowel (*a/gain*). It isn't possible to have a syllable that is a single consonant. Once the word has been broken into its component syllables the reader is able to study the syllables to find ones that are familiar and might give her a clue as to the word's meaning, such as certain prefixes or suffixes.

30. C: Phonological cues are based on the speech sounds in words and their alphabetic representations in print. Readers can identify words by knowing sound-to-letter correspondences. Syntactic cues (A) are based on how words are arranged and ordered to create meaningful phrases, clauses, and sentences. Semantic cues (B) are based on the meanings of morphemes and words and how they combine to create additional meanings. Pragmatic cues (D) are based on the readers' purposes for reading and their understanding of how textual structures function in the texts that they read.

31. B: Character development is not a common function of reading and writing; it is a skill set for a specific type of writing. Reading can achieve a variety of purposes. Initially, students learn to read as a form of language acquisition. This process also enables them to learn about various concepts through written texts, both inside and outside of school. Individuals will write and read to share thoughts, stories, and ideas with others. As language develops, many individuals will view reading as a common form of entertainment or enjoyment, regardless of the text's perceived instructional value or content.

32. B: This is an example of a closed question because it asks either/or and the student can only answer "simile" or "metaphor" without needing to elaborate unless asked to explain the answer. In contrast, choice C is an open-ended question because the student must both define simile and metaphor and explain the difference between them. Choice A is an open-ended literature question because the student cannot answer with yes, no, or some other single word or short phrase; s/he has to describe the action or events in a story that represent its climax, which requires understanding story structure, story elements, knowing the definition of a story's climax, reading the story, and understanding it. Choice D is a very open-ended question, as students have considerable latitude in giving the reasons each of them perceives for having poetry.

33. D: Prefixes, appearing at the beginning of base words to change their meanings. Suffixes appear at the end of words. Prefixes are attached to the beginning of words to change their meanings. *Un+happy, bi+monthly,* and *re+examine* are prefixes that, by definition, change the meanings of the words to which they are attached.

34. A: The process of actively constructing meaning from reading is interactive, in that it involves the text itself, the person reading it, and the setting in which the reading is done: the reader interacts with the text, and the text interacts with the reader by affecting him/her; the context of reading interacts with the text and the reader by affecting them both; and the reader interacts with the reading context as well as with the text. Choice B is a better definition of the *strategic* aspect of the process. Options C and D are better definitions of the *adaptable* aspect of the process.

35. A: In order to achieve a balanced language program, a teacher must spend time on many different skills that have been mentioned in previous questions and answers. Language skills cannot be reduced to the process of reading (fluency plus comprehension). Students develop their language skills over a long period of time, and they do so across multiple domains. Students' ability to listen and speak, write, view, respond, synthesize information, and read for a variety of purposes all must be included in daily instruction. By practicing only fluency and comprehension, students will not fully understand the various functions of language skills and may even lack an appreciation for them.

36. C: It is normal for students to reverse letters and numbers occasionally not only in 1st grade but through the end of 2nd grade. Thus, they do not indicate possible dyslexia (B) at this age. The words cited are above 1st-grade spelling level, particularly so early in the school year, so misspelling them is normal, should not be marked incorrect, and does not require intervention (D). Also, teachers should not deduct points for misspelling in written compositions unless the misspelled words are included in weekly class spelling lists. First-graders are frequently in transitional phases of writing when phonetic spelling is not only common but desirable. The student's writing is developmentally appropriate; the substitute's grading is inappropriate. Hence choice A is incorrect.

37. A: Cooperative learning and reading comprehension. Cooperative learning occurs when a group of students at various levels of reading ability have goals in common. Reading comprehension is achieved through reading both orally and silently, developing vocabulary, a reader's ability to predict what will occur in a piece of writing, a reader's ability to summarize the main points in a piece of writing, and a reader's ability to reflect on the text's meaning and connect that meaning to another text or personal experience.

38. B: As linguists have long pointed out, dialects are NOT non-standard versions of a language (A). In linguistics, dialects are *differing* varieties of any language, but these may be vernacular (nonstandard) OR standard versions of a language. They are often considered less socially acceptable, especially in educational, occupational and professional settings, than whichever standard version is most accepted. The linguistic features of dialects are not incorrect (C), but simply different. Their use does not indicate poor or incomplete language learning (D).

39. B: Integrated curriculum is vital to student growth and to fostering a love of learning. In reality, all subject areas are related, and a good teacher will find ways to highlight the connection of concepts across the curriculum. In choice B, the science teacher provides a way to help students study for a test. However, she would probably be better advised to work with the students on comprehension and retention before test time arrives. She could use a variety of previewing and reviewing skills, as well as creative ways to bring the information to life during class discussions and activities. This teacher might also benefit from discussing the situation with a language arts teacher to get ideas on how to build skills in reading for information, main ideas, and supporting concepts.

40. C: Because this student loves reading graphic novels and has both talent and enjoyment in drawing, having him create his own graphic novels is a good way to motivate him to write by using his visual style, ability, and interest to access writing activity. Giving audio recordings (A) to a highly visual student is not as appropriate to his strengths and interests. Letting him substitute drawing pictures for all writing assignments (B) would address his strengths and interests, but not his needs for learning to write. Having him watch animated videos about writing (D) would suit his visual learning style, but would not give him the actual writing practice he needs.

41. C: They meet to discuss areas the teacher is most concerned about and decide on the teacher's goals. In order to best achieve goals, those goals must be understood and established.

42. B: The word "brunch" is a blend of "breakfast" and "lunch". Blends of two or more words are known as portmanteau words. (*Portmanteau* is a French word meaning a suitcase.) "Fax" (A) is an example of clipping, or shortening a word, from its original "facsimile." "Babysitter" (C) is an example of compounding, or combining two or more words into one. "Saxophone" (D) is an example of proper noun

transfer: A Belgian family that built musical instruments had the last name of Sax, and this wind instrument was named after them. These represent some of the ways that new words have entered—and still do enter—the English language.

43. A: Most traditional methods teach reading via aural and visual techniques. However, students with auditory processing problems or dyslexia will not learn to read effectively with these methods, no matter how much practice is provided. Therefore, most students with this type of difficulty will benefit from a multi-sensory technique in which they can make use of all their senses. Combined with systematic instruction and a great deal of practice, the multi-sensory technique is very effective in building reading and processing skills in students with this kind of life-long learning difference.

44. A: This is an example of formative assessment, which can be formal or informal but is more often informal; it is conducted during instruction to inform teachers of student progress and enable them to adjust instruction if it is not effective enough; this is done on an ongoing basis. Summative assessment (B) is typically formal; it is conducted after instruction to measure final results for grading, promotion, accountability, etc. and inform changes to future instruction, but does not enable adjusting the current instruction. Therefore, it is not an example of choices C or D.

45. D: Round-robin reading is a common practice in language arts classes and has been for many years. In this process, students take turns reading aloud for their peers. Other students are asked to follow along silently in their texts while a peer is reading. This strategy does provide a way for students to read texts in class and include as many students as possible, which is often the intended outcome. However, this process often creates a boring atmosphere, since only one student at a time is actively engaged. While that student is reading, other students may become distracted by their own thoughts, other school work, or off-task interaction with each another; all of these issues subvert the intended outcome of the process. There is rarely enough time for each student to practice reading aloud to build students' reading fluency or comprehension in significant ways.

46. A: After prewriting (planning, visualizing, brainstorming), the correct sequence of steps in the writing process are drafting, in which the writer takes the material generated during prewriting work and making it into sentences and paragraphs; revising, where the writer explores any changes in what one has written that would improve the quality of the writing; editing, in which the writer examines his or her writing for factual and mechanical (grammar, spelling, punctuation) errors and correcting them; and publishing, when the writer finally shares what he or she has written with others who will read it and give feedback.

47. B: The term "blend" is commonly used to refer to a grapheme consisting of two sounds, such as the /fl/ in *flip*. In this word, the /f/ and /l/ sounds are distinctly audible. However, the words from the question prompt contain phoneme combinations in which a completely new sound is formed. The /ch/ sound is similar

to neither the /c/ nor /h/. This type of combination is called a "digraph," which is a kind of blended sound.

48. C: Because drawing a dodecagon and counting its diagonals is an arduous task, it is useful to employ a different problem-solving strategy. One such strategy is to draw polygons with fewer sides and look for a pattern in the number of the polygons' diagonals.

	3	0
	4	2
	5	5
	6	9
Heptagon	7	14
Octagon	8	20

A quadrilateral has two more diagonals than a triangle, a pentagon has three more diagonals than a quadrilateral, and a hexagon has four more diagonals than a pentagon. Continue this pattern to find that a dodecagon has 54 diagonals.

49. D: When the dress is marked down by 20%, the cost of the dress is 80% of its original price; thus, the reduced price of the dress can be written as $\frac{80}{100}x$, or $\frac{4}{5}x$, where x is the original price. When discounted an extra 25%, the dress costs 75% of the reduced price, or $\frac{75}{100}\left(\frac{4}{5}x\right)$, or $\frac{3}{4}\left(\frac{4}{5}x\right)$, which simplifies to $\frac{3}{5}x$. So the final price of the dress is three-fifths of the original price.

50. C: Aaron ran four miles from home and then back again, so he ran a total of eight miles. Therefore, statement III is false. Statements I and II, however, are both true. Since Aaron ran eight miles in eighty minutes, he ran an average of one mile every ten minutes, or six miles per hour; he ran two miles from point A to B in 20 minutes and four miles from D to E in 40 minutes, so his running speed between both sets of points was the same.

51. D: Since a and b are even integers, each can be expressed as the product of 2 and an integer. So, if we write $a = 2x$ and $b = 2y$, $3(2x)^2 + 9(2y)^3 = c$.
$$3(4x^2) + 9(8y^3) = c$$
$$12x^2 + 72y^3 = c$$
$$12(x^2 + 6y^3) = c$$

Since c is the product of 12 and some other integer, 12 must be a factor of c. Incidentally, the numbers 2, 3, and 6 must also be factors of c since each is also a factor of 12.

52. B: Notice that choice C cannot be correct since $x \neq 1$. ($x = 1$ results in a zero in the denominator.)

$$\frac{x-2}{x-1} = \frac{x-1}{x+1} + \frac{2}{x-1}$$
$$(x-1)(x+1)\left(\frac{x-2}{x-1} = \frac{x-1}{x+1} + \frac{2}{x-1}\right)$$
$$(x+1)(x-2) = (x-1)^2 + 2(x+1)$$
$$x^2 - x - 2 = x^2 - 2x + 1 + 2x + 2$$
$$x^2 - x - 2 = x^2 + 3$$
$$-x = 5$$
$$x = -5$$

53. B: A cube has six square faces. The arrangement of these faces in a two-dimensional figure is a net of a cube if the figure can be folded to form a cube. Figures A, C, and D represent three of the eleven possible nets of a cube. If choice B is folded, however, the bottom square in the second column will overlap the fourth square in the top row, so the figure does not represent a net of a cube.

54. D: The point $(5, -5)$ lies on the line which has a slope of -2 and which passes through $(3, -1)$. If $(5, -5)$ is one of the endpoints of the line, the other would be

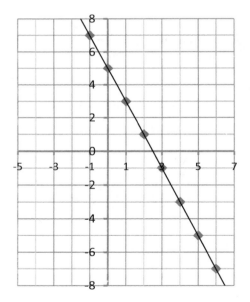

$(1,3)$.

55. B: The manufacturer wishes to minimize the surface area A of the can while keeping its volume V fixed at $0.5 \text{ L} = 500 \text{ mL} = 500 \text{ cm}^3$. The formula for the

surface area of a cylinder is $A = 2\pi rh + 2\pi r^2$, and the formula for volume is $V = \pi r^2 h$. To combine the two formulas into one, solve the volume formula for r or h and substitute the resulting expression into the surface area formula for r or h. The volume of the cylinder is 500 cm^3, so $500 = \pi r^2 h \rightarrow h = \frac{500}{\pi r^2}$. Therefore, $A = 2\pi rh + 2\pi r^2 \rightarrow 2\pi r\left(\frac{500}{\pi r^2}\right) + 2\pi r^2 = \frac{1000}{r} + 2\pi r^2$. Find the critical point(s) by setting the first derivative equal to zero and solving for r. Note that r represents the radius of the can and must therefore be a positive number.

$$A = 1000r^{-1} + 2\pi r^2$$
$$A' = -1000r^{-2} + 4\pi r$$
$$0 = -\frac{1000}{r^2} + 4\pi r$$
$$\frac{1000}{r^2} = 4\pi r$$
$$1000 = 4\pi r^3$$
$$\sqrt[3]{\frac{1000}{4\pi}} = r$$

So, when r≈4.3 cm, the minimum surface area is obtained. When the radius of the can is 4.30 cm, its height is $h \approx \frac{500}{\pi(4.30)^2} \approx 8.6$ cm, and the surface area is approximately $\frac{1000}{4.3} + 2\pi(4.3)^2 \approx 348.73$ cm^2.

Confirm that the surface area is greater when the radius is slightly smaller or larger than 4.3 cm. For instance, when r=4 cm, the surface area is approximately 350.5 cm^2, and when r=4.5 cm, the surface area is approximately 349.5 cm^2.

56. C: When rolling two dice, there is only one way to roll a sum of two (rolling a 1 on each die) and twelve (rolling 6 on each die). In contrast, there are two ways to obtain a sum of three (rolling a 2 and 1 or a 1 and 2) and eleven (rolling a 5 and 6 or a 6 and 5), three ways to obtain a sum of four (1 and 3; 2 and 2; 3 and 1) or ten (4 and 6; 5 and 5; 6 and 4), and so on. Since the probability of obtaining each sum is inconsistent, choice C is not an appropriate simulation. Choice A is acceptable since the probability of picking A, 1, 2, 3, 4, 5, 6, 7, 8, 9, or J from the modified deck cards of cards is equally likely, each with a probability of $\frac{4}{52-8} = \frac{4}{44} = \frac{1}{11}$. Choice B is also acceptable since the computer randomly generates one number from eleven possible numbers, so the probability of generating any of the numbers is $\frac{1}{11}$.

57. A: If a number is divisible by 2 and 3, it is also divisible by the lowest common multiple of these two factors. The lowest common multiple of 2 and 3 is their product, 6.

58. C. The original price may be modeled by the equation, $(x - 0.45x) + 0.0875(x - 0.45x) = 39.95$, which simplifies to $0.598125x = 39.95$. Dividing each side of the equation by the coefficient of x gives $x \approx 66.79$.

59. C: An inverse proportional relationship is written in the form $y = \frac{k}{x}$, thus the equation $y = \frac{3}{x}$ shows that y is inversely proportional to x.

60. C: Using the points $(-3, 1)$ and $(1, -11)$, the slope may be written as $m = \frac{-11-1}{1-(-3)}$ or $m = -3$. Substituting the slope of -3 and the x- and y-values from the point $(-3, 1)$, into the slope-intercept form of an equation gives $1 = -3(-3) + b$, which simplifies to $1 = 9 + b$. Subtracting 9 from both sides of the equation gives $b = -8$. Thus, the linear equation that includes the data in the table is $y = -3x - 8$.

61. A: The inequality will be less than or equal to, since he may spend \$100 or less on his purchase.

62. C: The surface area of a sphere may be calculated using the formula $SA = 4\pi r^2$. Substituting 9 for r gives $SA = 4\pi(9)^2$, which simplifies to $SA \approx 1017.36$. So the surface area of the ball is approximately 1017.36 square inches. There are twelve inches in a foot, so there are $12^2 = 144$ square inches in a square foot. In order to convert this measurement to square feet, then, the following proportion may be written and solved for x: $\frac{1}{144} = \frac{x}{1017.36}$. So $x \approx 7.07$. He needs approximately 7.07 square feet of wrapping paper.

63. C: The original triangle was reflected across the x-axis. When reflecting across the x-axis, the x-values of each point remain the same, but the y-values of the points will be opposites. $(1, 4) \rightarrow (1, -4), (5, \ 4) \rightarrow (5, -4), (3, 8) \rightarrow (3, -8)$.

64. B: The probability may be written as $P(E \text{ and } H) = P(E) \cdot P(H)$. Substituting the probability of each event gives $(E \text{ and } H) = \frac{1}{2} \cdot \frac{1}{2}$, which simplifies to $\frac{1}{4}$.

65. B: This is a formative assessment because she is assessing students while she is still teaching the unit. Summative assessments are given at the end of the unit. Formal assessments are usually a quizzes or tests. Informal assessments include asking individual students questions. Therefore, the correct choice is B.

66. A: Choice A is correct because standards for fourth grade state that students will be able to use a protractor to determine the approximate measures of angles in degrees to the nearest whole number. Choices B, C, and D are stated in the standards for fifth grade. Therefore, the correct choice is A.

67. B: Sophia needs to find multiples of 3 (3, 6, 9, 12, 15...) and multiples of 4 (4, 8, 12, 16,...) and find the least common multiple between them, which is 12. The greatest common divisor of 3 and 4 is 1. The least common divisor between two numbers is always 1. The greatest common multiple can never be determined. Therefore, the correct choice is B.

68. D: Number lines can help students understand the concepts of positive and negative numbers. Fraction strips are most commonly used with fractions. Venn diagrams are commonly used when comparing groups. Shaded regions are commonly used with fractions or percentages. Therefore, the correct choice is D.

69. C: The associative property of multiplication states that when three or more numbers are multiplied, the product is the same regardless of the way in which the numbers are grouped. Choice C shows that the product of 2, 3, and 4 is the same with two different groupings of the factors. Choice A demonstrates the distributive property. Choice B shows grouping, but the factors are different. Choice D demonstrates the commutative property of multiplication. Therefore, the correct choice is C.

70. B: The equation $y + 3 = 7$ is solved by subtracting 3 from both sides to yield $y = 4$.
Substituting $y = 4$ into $x - 1 = y$ yields $x - 1 = 4$. Adding 1 to both sides of this equation yields $x = 5$. Therefore, the correct choice is B.

71. C: Triangles can be classified as scalene, isosceles, or equilateral. Scalene triangles have no equal side measurements and no equal angle measurements. Isosceles triangles have two sides of equal measurement and two angles of equal measurement. Equilateral triangles have three sides of equal measurement and three angles of equal measurement. A right triangle is isosceles only if its two acute angles are congruent. Therefore, the correct choice is C.

72. C: The slope of a line can be found from any two points by the formula $slope = \frac{y_2 - y_1}{x_2 - x_1}$. A quick sketch of the point in choice C reveals a line with a negative slope. Substituting the last two points into the formula yields $slope = \frac{-3 - 1}{0 - (-6)}$ which reduces to $\frac{-4}{6}$ or $\frac{-2}{3}$. The points in choice A form a line with a positive slope. The points in choice B form a line with a negative slope of $\frac{-3}{2}$. The points in choice D form a horizontal line. Therefore, the correct choice is C.

73. C: The mean is the average of the data and can be found by dividing the sum of the data by the number of data: $\frac{16 + 18 + 20 + 21 + 34 + 45 + 49}{7} = 29$. The median is the middle data point when the data are ranked numerically. The median is 21. Therefore, the correct choice is C.

74. B: The histogram only shows that there are eight trees between 70 and 75 feet tall. It does not show the individual heights of the trees. That information cannot be obtained from this graph. Therefore, the correct choice is B.

75. A: To a convert a percent to a fraction, remove the percent sign and place the number over 100. That means 15% can be written as $\frac{15}{100}$, which reduces to $\frac{3}{20}$. To

- 109 -

covert a percent to a decimal, remove the percent sign and move the decimal two places to the left. To convert a percent to a ratio, first write the ratio as a fraction, and then rewrite the fraction as a ratio. Therefore, the correct choice is A.

76. C. The number 589 can be estimated to be 600. The number 9 can be estimated to be 10. The number of chicken nuggets is approximately 600×10, which is 6,000 nuggets. Therefore, the correct choice is C.

77. D: The total rainfall is 25.38 inches. Thus, the ratio $\frac{4.5}{25.38}$, represents the percentage of rainfall received during October. $\frac{4.5}{25.38} \approx 0.177$ or 17.7%.

78. C: The volume of a cylinder may be calculated using the formula $V = \pi r^2 h$, where r represents the radius and h represents the height. Substituting 1.5 for r and 3 for h gives $V = \pi(1.5)^2(3)$, which simplifies to $V \approx 21.2$.

79. D: The area of the square is equal to $(30)^2$, or 900 square centimeters. The area of the circle is equal to $\pi(15)^2$, or approximately 707 square centimeters. The area of the shaded region is equal to the difference of the area of the square and the area of the circle, or 900 cm² – 707 cm², which equals 193 cm². So the area of the shaded region is about 193 cm².

80. B: The perimeter is equal to the sum of the lengths of the two bases, 2 and 6 units, and the diagonal distances of the other two sides. Using the distance formula, each side length may be represented as $d = \sqrt{20} = 2\sqrt{5}$. Thus, the sum of the two sides is equal to $2\sqrt{20}$, or $4\sqrt{5}$. The whole perimeter is equal to $8 + 4\sqrt{5}$.

81. C: The slope may be written as $m = \frac{4-0}{-3-(-4)}$, which simplifies to $m = 4$.

82. A: $A \cap B$ means "A intersect B," or the elements that are common to both sets. "A intersect B" represents "A and B," that is, an element is in the intersection of A and B if it is in A *and* it is in B. The elements 2, 5, and 8 are common to both sets.

83. C: To find the probability of an event, divide the number of favorable outcomes by the total number of outcomes. When there are two events in which the first depends on the second, multiply the first ratio by the second ratio. In the first part of the problem, the probability of choosing a licorice jelly bean is two out of twenty possible outcomes, or $\frac{2}{20}$. Then, because one jelly bean has already been chosen, there are four cinnamon beans out of a total of 19, or $\frac{4}{19}$. By multiplying the two ratios and dividing by a common denominator, one arrives at the final probability of $\frac{2}{95}$.

84. C: There are 36 months in 3 years. The following proportion may be written: $\frac{450}{3} = \frac{x}{36}$. The equation $3x = 16200$, may be solved for x. Dividing both sides of the equation by 3 gives $x = 5,400$.

85. A: It is not true that England's defeat of the Spanish Armada in 1588 ended their war with Spain. It did establish England's naval dominance and strengthened England's future colonization of the New World, but the actual war between England and Spain did not end until 1604. It is true that Henry VIII's desire to divorce Catherine of Aragon strengthened English expansionism (B). Catherine was Spanish, and Henry split from the Catholic Church because it prohibited divorce. Henry's rejection of his Spanish wife and his subsequent support of the Protestant movement angered King Philip II of Spain and destroyed the formerly close ties between the two countries. When Elizabeth became Queen of England, she supported the Reformation as a Protestant, which also contributed to English colonization (C). Sir Francis Drake, one of the best known English sea captains during this time period, would attack and plunder Spanish ships that had plundered American Indians (D), adding to the enmity between Spain and England. Queen Elizabeth invested in Drake's voyages and gave him her support in claiming territories for England.

86. A: The latest occurring decolonization event was the Eastern Bloc and Soviet Satellite states of Armenia, Azerbaijan, Estonia, Georgia, Kazakhstan, Kyrgyzstan, Latvia, Lithuania, Moldova, Russia, Tajikistan, Turkmenistan, Ukraine, and Uzbekistan all became independent from the Soviet Union in 1991. (Note: This was the last decolonization of the Cold War years, as the end of the Soviet Union marked the end of the Cold War.) Canada completed its independence from British Parliament via the Canada Act (B) in 1982. In the Caribbean, the Bahamas gained independence from the United Kingdom (C) in 1973. Algeria won its independence from France when the Algerian War of Independence, begun in 1954, ended in 1962 (D). In Africa, Libya gained independence from Italy and became an independent kingdom in 1951.

87. A: The President has the authority to negotiate and sign treaties. A two-thirds vote of the Senate, however, is needed to ratify a treaty for it to be upheld.

88. C: Article III judges are appointed for life and can retire at 65. They can only be removed from their posts by impeachment in the House and conviction in the Senate. Having judges serve life terms is meant to allow them to serve without being governed by the changing opinions of the public.

89. B: "...endowed by their Creator with certain unalienable Rights," is excerpted from the Declaration of Independence. These rights are unable to be taken away from individuals, referring to the colonists' rights that Great Britain could not oppress.

90. D: It is not true that the Gilded Age is a term whose origins have not been identified clearly. In 1873, Mark Twain and Charles Dudley Warner co-authored a book entitled The Gilded Age: A Tale of Today. Twain and Warner first coined this term to describe the extravagance and excesses of America's wealthy upper class (B), who became richer than ever due to industrialization. Furthermore, the Gilded Age was the era of the "robber barons" (A) such as John D. Rockefeller, Cornelius Vanderbilt, J.P. Morgan, and others. Because they accumulated enormous wealth through extremely aggressive and occasionally unethical monetary manipulations, critics dubbed them "robber barons" because they seemed to be elite lords of robbery. While these business tycoons grasped huge fortunes, some of them—such as Andrew Carnegie and Andrew Mellon—were also philanthropists, using their wealth to support and further worthy causes such as literacy, education, health care, charities, and the arts. They donated millions of dollars to fund social improvements. Carnegie himself dubbed this large philanthropic movement the "Gospel of Wealth" (C). Another characteristic of the Gilded Age was the Beaux Arts architectural style, a neo-Renaissance style modeled after the great architectural designs of the European Renaissance. The Panic of 1893 ended the Gilded and began a severe four-year economic depression. The Progressive Era followed these events.

91. A: One example of the multiplier effect of large cities would be if the presence of specialized equipment for an industry attracted even more business. Large cities tend to grow even larger for a number of reasons: they have more skilled workers, they have greater concentrations of specialized equipment, and they have already-functioning markets. These factors all make it easier for a business to begin operations in a large city than elsewhere. Thus, the populations and economic productivity of large cities tend to grow quickly. Some governments have sought to mitigate this trend by clustering groups of similar industries in smaller cities.

92. D: Criminal cases are tried under both state law and federal law. The nature of the crime determines whether it is tried in state court or federal court.

93. D: The Louisiana Purchase actually increased the U.S.'s territory by 100% overnight, not 10%. The Louisiana territory doubled the size of the nation. It is true that Jefferson initially sent a delegation to Paris to see if Napoleon would agree to sell only New Orleans to the United States (A). It is also true that Napoleon, who expected America to encroach on Louisiana, decided to avoid this by offering to sell the entire territory to the U.S. (B). It is likewise true that America only had authority to buy New Orleans. Nevertheless, the delegation accepted Napoleon's offer of all of Louisiana (C). Due to his belief in a strict interpretation of the Constitution, Jefferson did require approval from Congress to make the purchase. When his advisors characterized the purchase as being within his purview based on the presidential power to make treaties, Congress agreed.

94. C: Mercantilism is the economic theory that nations advance the goal of accumulating capital by maintaining a balance of trade such that the value of exports exceeds that of imports. Great Britain maintained colonies to provide an inexpensive

source of raw materials while creating markets for the goods manufactured in England. Under free trade, governments refrain from hindering the international exchange of goods and services. Nations that are granted most favored nation status are assured of enjoying equal advantages in international trade. A laissez-faire capitalist economy would theoretically be completely free of government regulation.

95. B: During the early Medieval period (or Middle Ages), Europe was characterized by widespread illiteracy, ignorance, and superstition once the unifying influence of the Roman Empire was lost. Few universities, like the university at Constantinople founded in 2 C.E. and those at Athens, Antioch, and Alexandria around the same time, existed then. Before the 5th and 6th centuries C.E., any education was conducted at cathedral or monastery schools or privately in the homes of wealthy families, which cannot be considered "main centers of literacy." More religious schools were created through Charlemagne's reforms in the 9th century, and early forms of universities began developing in the 11th and 12th centuries.

96. A: The Supreme Court interprets law and the Constitution. The inferior courts are bound to uphold the law as the Supreme Court interprets and rules on it.

97. B: Members of the House of Representatives are elected in proportion to the population of each state. Representation by senators is not based on population and is therefore skewed in electoral weight. The Electoral College can and has contradicted the popular vote in the Presidential election.

98. D: Federalists who helped frame the Constitution believed the central government needed to be stronger than what was established under the Articles of Confederation. Anti-federalists were against this and feared a strong federal government. A system of checks and balances was established to prevent the central government from taking too much power.

99. B: James Madison was a close friend of Thomas Jefferson and supported a stronger central government. George Mason and Robert Yates were both against expanding federal authority over the states. Benjamin Franklin was a proponent of a strong federal government, but he was from Massachusetts.

100. C: When a nation follows the theory of comparative advantage, it specializes in producing the goods and services it can make at a lower opportunity cost and then engages in trade to obtain other goods.

101. A: Presidents may veto legislation passed by both houses of Congress, and in turn, Congress can override a Presidential veto with a 2/3 majority. These governmental practices are a further manifestation that each branch of government is watched by the other branches and, when necessary, can undo a decision it deems ill-advised or unconstitutional.

102. B: The House has strict rules that limit debate. A filibuster can only occur in the Senate where Senators can speak on topics other than the bill at hand and introduce amendments. A filibuster can be ended by a supermajority vote of 60 Senators.

103. C: The President must be a natural citizen, be at least 35 years old, and have lived in the U.S. for 14 years. There is no education requirement for becoming President. Truman did not have a college education, but most Presidents have degrees.

104. C: A person who has taken out a fixed-rate loan can benefit from inflation by paying back the loan with dollars that are less valuable than they were when the loan was taken out. In the other examples, inflation harms the individual or entity.

105. B: Growth of industry was concentrated in urban areas, which cyclically drew laborers into cities, growing the population of cities and increasing efficiency and quality in industry.

106. B: Oligarchy is defined as the rule by few. An example is aristocracy, which in ancient Greece, was government by an elite group of citizens as opposed to a monarchy. In later times, it meant government by the class of aristocrats, a privileged group, as opposed to democracy. The rule of one is called autocracy. Examples include monarchy, dictatorship, and many others. The rule by law is called a republic. Some examples are constitutional republics, parliamentary republics, and federal republics. The rule by many could apply to democracy, which governs according to the people's votes or to the collective leadership form of socialism, where no one individual has too much power.

107. B: The Trail of Tears was the forcible removal of Native American tribes from their homes in the Southeastern US to Oklahoma. The name came due to the high number of Native Americans who died on the journey.

108. B: Tropical regions near the Equator tend to experience relatively constant temperatures year-round because the angle at which sunlight hits them remains relatively constant throughout the year. In regions that are farther north or south, the angle at which sunlight hits them changes much more drastically due to the changing angle of the Earth's axis relative to the Sun. This results in greater variations in the length of daylight and in temperatures. Tropical regions do have seasons (usually a "wet" season and a "dry" season), but temperature fluctuations are less pronounced than those in regions farther from the Equator.

109. B: In order to prosper, a nation should not try to increase its imports. Mercantilism is an economic theory including the idea that prosperity comes from a positive balance of international trade. For any one nation to prosper, that nation should increase its exports (C) but decrease its imports. Exporting more to other countries while importing less from them will give a country a positive trade balance. This theory assumes that money and wealth are identical (A) assets of a

nation. In addition, this theory also assumes that the volume of global trade is an unchangeable quantity. Mercantilism dictates that a nation's government should apply a policy of economic protectionism (D) by stimulating more exports and suppressing imports. Some ways to accomplish this task have included granting subsidies for exports and imposing tariffs on imports. Mercantilism can be regarded as essentially the opposite of the free trade policies that have been encouraged in more recent years.

110. C: Copernicus's De Revolutionibus orbium coelestium (On the Revolutions of the Heavenly Spheres) was published in 1543, almost simultaneously with his death. He was the first to contradict the then-accepted belief that the Earth was the center of the universe and the Sun and other bodies moved around it. This geocentric model was associated with Ptolemy and hence called the Ptolemaic system. Galileo Galilei published Siderius Nuncius (Starry Messenger) in 1610. In it, he revealed his observations, made through his improvements to the telescope, which corroborated Copernicus's theory. Sir Isaac Newton (1642–1727) built the first usable reflecting telescope and erased any lingering doubts about a heliocentric universe by describing universal gravitation and showing its congruence with Kepler's laws of planetary motion.

111. B: Members of the House are elected for two-year terms. Senators serve six-year terms, but the elections are staggered so roughly one-third of the Senate is elected every two years.

112. A: A city located at 6,000 feet above sea level is likely to have a cooler climate, all other things being equal. Since air is less dense at higher altitudes, it holds heat less effectively and temperatures tend to be lower as a result. Precipitation is not as strong an indicator of temperature. Some areas that receive moderate or large amounts of precipitation are cooler (temperate and continental climates), while some areas that receive lots of precipitation, like the tropics, are warmer.

113. D: Niccolò Machiavelli, perhaps best known for his book The Prince, was an Italian Renaissance political philosopher noted for writing more realistic representations and rational interpretations of politics. In The Prince, he popularized the political concept of "the ends justify the means." Dante Alighieri was a great poet famous for his Commedia (additionally labeled Divina by contemporary poet and author Bocaccio, who wrote the Decameron and other works) or Divine Comedy, a trilogy consisting of Inferno, Purgatorio, and Paradiso (Hell, Purgatory, and Heaven). Dante's work helped propel the transition from the Medieval period to the Renaissance. Francesco Petrarca, known in English as Petrarch, was famous for his lyrical poetry, particularly sonnets.

114. A: A good hypothesis is testable and logical, and can be used to predict future events. A good hypothesis is also simple, not complex. Therefore, the correct choice is A.

115. A: They will be refracted and converge. When light waves hit a convex lens they are refracted and converge. A convex lens curves or bulges with the middle being thicker and the edges thinner. A magnifying glass is an example. Light rays are refracted by different amounts as they pass through the lens. After light rays pass through, they converge at a point called the focus. An object viewed with a magnifying glass looks bigger because the lens bends the rays inwards. Choice B would indicate a concave lens as it would cause the light to be refracted and diverge. Light is not reflected in this case, so neither choice C nor D would be applicable.

116. D: Circulatory System – exchanges gasses with the environment by delivering oxygen to the bloodstream and releasing carbon dioxide, is not paired correctly. It is the respiratory system that exchanges gasses with the environment by delivering oxygen to the bloodstream and releasing carbon dioxide. The circulatory system transports nutrients, gasses, hormones, and blood to and away from cells. The muscle system controls movement through three types of muscle tissue. The nervous system controls sensory responses by carrying impulses away from and toward the cell body. The digestive system breaks down food for absorption into the blood stream where it is delivered to cells for respiration.

117. A: The addition of energy causes a phase change. Phase changes are physical changes, not chemical changes. While sublimation is an example of a phase change, it occurs when a solid turns directly into a gas without passing through the liquid state. Condensation, another phase change, occurs when a gas turns to liquid.

118. A: Dispose of the solutions according to local disposal procedures. Solutions and compounds used in labs may be hazardous according to state and local regulatory agencies and should be treated with such precaution. Emptying the solutions into the sink and rinsing with warm water and soap does not take into account the hazards associated with a specific solution in terms of vapors or interactions with water, soap, and waste piping systems. Ensuring the solutions are secured in closed containers and throwing them away may allow toxic chemicals into landfills and subsequently into fresh water systems. Storing the solutions in a secured, dry place for later use is incorrect as chemicals should not be re-used due to the possibility of contamination.

119. D: The atomic number is equal to the number of electrons. An atom has a neutral charge if its atomic number is equal to its number of electrons. The atomic number (Z) of an element refers to the number of protons in the nucleus. If an atom has fewer or more electrons than its atomic number, then it will be positively or negatively charged, respectively. Cations are positively charged ions; anions are negatively charged ones. Choices A and B both describe a nucleus containing only neutrons with no protons. An element of this nature is referred to as neutronium but is theoretical only.

120. C: Transform. Transform is not connected to the process of mountain building. Orogeny, or mountain building, occurs at the Earth's lithosphere or crust. Folding, or deformation, is a process that occurs to make mountains where two portions of the lithosphere collide. One is subducted and the other is pushed upward forming a mountain. This action produces various types of folding. Faulting can be characterized by a brittle deformation where the rock breaks abruptly (compared with folding). Faulting and fault types are associated with earthquakes and relatively rapid deformation. Convergent is a more general term used to describe plates interacting.

121. A: Repeating a measurement several times can increase the accuracy of the measurement. Calibrating the equipment (B) will increase the precision of the measurement. None of the other choices are useful strategies to increase the accuracy of a measurement.

122. B: Refractive Index. The refractive index is an optical property which is not related to the organization of the periodic table. Elements on the periodic table are arranged into periods, or rows, according to atomic number, which is the number of protons in the nucleus. The periodic table illustrates the recurrence of properties. Each column, or group, contains elements that share similar properties, such as reactivity.

123. C: The pressure decreases to one-third. A gas in a closed container at constant temperature will decrease in pressure to one-third when the volume of the container is tripled. The ideal gas law is $PV = nRT$ where P is pressure, V is volume, n is the moles of the gas, R is the gas constant and T is temperature. A variation to solve for pressure is: $P = nRT/V$. Boyle's Law indicates that pressure and volume are inversely proportional. The pressure cannot be increased because that would imply that pressure and volume are directly proportional.

124. C: Laccolith. A laccolith is formed when an intrusion of magma injected between two layers of sedimentary rock forces the overlying strata upward to create a dome-like form. Eventually, the magma cools, the sedimentary rock wears away and the formation is exposed. Sills and dikes are both examples of sheet intrusions, where magma has inserted itself into other rock. Sills are horizontal and dikes are vertical. A caldera is a crater-like feature that was formed from the collapse of a volcano after erupting.

125. C: For an experiment to be considered successful, it must yield data that others can reproduce. Choice A may be considered part of a well-designed experiment. Choices B and D may be considered part of an experiment that is reported on by individuals with expertise.

126. C: Heat transfer can never occur from a cooler object to a warmer object. While the second law of thermodynamics implies that heat never spontaneously transfers from a cooler object to a warmer object, it is possible for heat to be transferred to a warmer object, given the proper input of work to the system. This is the principle by which a refrigerator operates. Work is done to the system to transfer heat from the objects inside the refrigerator to the air surrounding the refrigerator. All other answer choices are true.

127. B: Light travels faster in air than it does in water. When the light travels from the wallet to the man, it will bend as it exits the water. The bending of light is called refraction and creates the illusion of the wallet being next to where it actually is.

128. C: The closer the data points are to each other, the more precise the data. This does not mean the data is accurate, but that the results are very reproducible.

129. D: The most recently formed parts of the Earth's crust can be found at mid-ocean ridges. New crust forms here when magma erupts from these ridges and

pushes pre-existing crust horizontally towards the continental plates. Such ridges include the Mid-Atlantic Ridge and the East Pacific Rise.

130. A: Fission. Fission is a nuclear process where atomic nuclei split apart to form smaller nuclei. Nuclear fission can release large amounts of energy, emit gamma rays and form daughter products. It is used in nuclear power plants and bombs. Answer B, Fusion, refers to a nuclear process whereby atomic nuclei join to form a heavier nucleus, such as with stars. This can release or absorb energy depending upon the original elements. Answer C, Decay, refers to an atomic nucleus spontaneously losing energy and emitting ionizing particles and radiation. Answer D, Ionization, refers to a process by which atoms obtain a positive or negative charge because the number of electrons does not equal that of protons.

131. C: The vapor pressure decreases by an amount proportional to the amount of solute. Raoult's law states that the vapor pressure of a solution containing a non-volatile solute is equal to the vapor pressure of the volatile solvent multiplied by its mole fraction, which is basically the proportion of the solution that is made up by solvent. In a liquid, some of the surface particles have higher than average energy and can break away to become a gas, or evaporate. The pressure of this gas right above the surface of the liquid is called the vapor pressure. Increasing the amount of solute in a liquid decreases the number of solvent particles at the surface. Because of this, fewer solvent molecules are able to escape, thus lowering the vapor pressure.

132. A: The prevailing westerlies. The prevailing westerlies drive weather systems to move west to east in the mid-latitudes. The direction refers to that which the wind is coming from. The polar easterlies that travel from the northeast occur between 90-60 degrees north latitude. The ones from the southeast are between 90-60 degrees south latitude. The trade winds refer to those occurring near the equator in the tropics moving east. The doldrums are also in the tropics but refer to an area of low-pressure where frequently the winds are light and unpredictable.

133. A: Many organisms, especially organisms that live in harsh conditions such as deserts or frozen icy areas, have developed specific adaptations that allow them to survive. For example, cacti are able to expand to store large amounts of water, coyotes absorb some water from their food, and snakes can escape the heat by hiding within rocks.

134. D: Mario balances a book on his head. In this example, work is not applied to the book because the book is not moving. One definition of work is a force acting on an object to cause displacement. In this case, the book was not displaced by the force applied to it. Mario's head applied a vertical force to the book to keep it in the same position.

135. D: Reproductive habits. Reproductive habits would not be considered evidence for evolution. Usually, how a species reproduces does not support nor add to the body of evidence for the theory of evolution. Reproduction habits might exemplify how any given organism can adapt to changes in its environment as a way to survive. This does not necessarily show evolution. Fossil record is evidence for evolution as it shows evolutionary change of organisms over time. DNA sequences show that organisms that are related evolutionarily also have related gene sequences. Anatomical structures such as having an internal bony structure provide evidence of descent from a common ancestor.

136. A: Glass. Glass is considered a non-renewable resource. Glass is manufactured and can be recycled, but is considered a non-renewable resource. Wood is considered a renewable resource because with proper management, an equilibrium can be reached between harvesting trees and planting new ones. Cattle are managed in herds and a balance can be achieved between those consumed and those born. Soil is the result of long-term erosion and includes organic matter and minerals needed by plants. Soil found naturally in the environment is renewed. Crops can be rotated to help maintain a healthy soil composition for farming.

137. A: The stream of charged particles that escape the Sun's gravitational pull is called solar wind. Solar wind is comprised primarily of protons and electrons, and these particles are deflected away from the Earth by its magnetic field. When stray particles do manage to enter the atmosphere, they cause the aurorae (Northern and Southern Lights) and geomagnetic storms that can affect power grids.

138. B: Voltage and current are directly proportional to one another. Ohm's Law states that voltage and current in an electrical circuit are directly proportional to one another. Ohm's Law can be expressed as V=IR, where V is voltage, I is current and R is resistance. Voltage is also known as electrical potential difference and is the force that moves electrons through a circuit. For a given amount of resistance, an increase in voltage will result in an increase in current. Resistance and current are inversely proportional to each other. For a given voltage, an increase in resistance will result in a decrease in current.

139. C: Flowers. Flowers are the reproductive organs of a plant. Flowering plants reproduce by sexual reproduction where the gametes join to form seeds. Pollen is sperm. Pollinators help transfer the sperm to the ovule, the egg. The style is the part of the female reproduction system that transports the sperm between the stigma and the ovary, all part of the pistil. The stigma is the sticky tip of the style on which the pollen lands. Sepals are usually small leaves between or underneath the petals and are not as obvious or as large and colorful as the petals.

140. B: Work is defined as the force used to move a mass over a distance. Choice A may be a secular (non-scientific) definition of work. Choice C is the definition of power. Choice D is the definition of potential energy.

141. D: Endocytosis is a process by which cells absorb larger molecules or even tiny organisms, such as bacteria, that would not be able to pass through the plasma membrane. Endocytic vesicles containing molecules from the extracellular environment often undergo further processing once they enter the cell.

142. B: Dimension, texture, and space are all *elements* of art, while unity is one of the *principles* of art. Unity in artwork is achieved when an artist's use of the elements produces a sense of wholeness or completeness in the finished product.

143. A: Drybrush is a technique that is primarily used in watercolor painting. It involves using a fine, nearly dry brush that is dipped in undiluted watercolor paint. It is used to

create precise brushstrokes—an effect that is otherwise very difficult to achieve in this medium.

144. A: A social studies lesson on political propaganda could be incorporated into an art class by asking students to evaluate political propaganda posters or create their own. Although the other lessons could possibly be incorporated, such an endeavor would not be particularly useful.

145. B: Because they lack a tonal center. For example, diminished triads consisting of a root, a minor third, and a diminished fifth symmetrically divide the octave. Choice A is incorrect since diminished chords do not necessarily sound "sad" depending on their placement in the chord progression (minor chords typically are considered "sad," anyway). Choice C, they are barely audible, is incorrect, as the word "diminished" refers to the state of the fifth and not the volume of the chord, which can be played at any volume. Finally, Choice D is incorrect, as diminished chords have been used throughout musical history in many famous works.

146. C: Value is the term that refers to the relative lightness or darkness of the colors in a painting. Intensity relates the vibrancy of colors in a painting; high-intensity colors are pure, while low-intensity colors are mixed with other colors to suggest a somber mood. A color's hue refers to the actual pigmentation (red, blue, green, or yellow). Texture is a tactile quality of an artwork's surface, rather than a property of color.

147. B: Line is the artistic element most commonly used to create the illusion of depth in a painting. For instance, an artist could use line to convey depth by incorporating an object, such as a road, that stretches from the foreground to the background of a painting. Balance is a principle of art that involves creating an impression of stability in a work; contrast and symmetry would not function to create the illusion of depth.

148. B: The activity, Musical hoops, is played like musical chairs, except children must jump into hoops instead of sitting on chairs when the music stops. This is appropriate for younger children. Freeze tag or blob tag (A) is more appropriate for children older than 5 years, up to 12 years old. Children must try to tag others while holding hands with those in their blob. This demands higher levels of coordination than younger children have. Follow the leader (C) is better as a warm-up activity for children age 5 to 12 years, as younger children can have difficulty with leading and following and with the variations in leaders and locomotor skills that teachers can use with older children. Therefore, choice D is incorrect.

149. A: Unsafe water is a risk factor for many diseases, but not for all four types of diseases listed. Drinking alcohol (B), poor nutrition (C), and smoking tobacco (D) are all risk factors shared in common by all four types of illnesses that cause the majority of deaths from noncommunicable diseases.

150. A: The advantage of drawing with charcoal as opposed to lead pencils is that charcoal can be smudged to create shading. Because of its loose, chalky texture, charcoal requires a

fixative, unlike lead pencil. Neither pencils nor charcoal is available in different hues, but both can be purchased in a range of values.

Secret Key #1 - Time is Your Greatest Enemy

Pace Yourself

Wear a watch. At the beginning of the test, check the time (or start a chronometer on your watch to count the minutes), and check the time after every few questions to make sure you are "on schedule."

If you are forced to speed up, do it efficiently. Usually one or more answer choices can be eliminated without too much difficulty. Above all, don't panic. Don't speed up and just begin guessing at random choices. By pacing yourself, and continually monitoring your progress against your watch, you will always know exactly how far ahead or behind you are with your available time. If you find that you are one minute behind on the test, don't skip one question without spending any time on it, just to catch back up. Take 15 fewer seconds on the next four questions, and after four questions you'll have caught back up. Once you catch back up, you can continue working each problem at your normal pace.

Furthermore, don't dwell on the problems that you were rushed on. If a problem was taking up too much time and you made a hurried guess, it must be difficult. The difficult questions are the ones you are most likely to miss anyway, so it isn't a big loss. It is better to end with more time than you need than to run out of time.

Lastly, sometimes it is beneficial to slow down if you are constantly getting ahead of time. You are always more likely to catch a careless mistake by working more slowly than quickly, and among very high-scoring test takers (those who are likely to have lots of time left over), careless errors affect the score more than mastery of material.

Secret Key #2 - Guessing is not Guesswork

You probably know that guessing is a good idea - unlike other standardized tests, there is no penalty for getting a wrong answer. Even if you have no idea about a question, you still have a 20-25% chance of getting it right.

Most test takers do not understand the impact that proper guessing can have on their score. Unless you score extremely high, guessing will significantly contribute to your final score.

Monkeys Take the Test

What most test takers don't realize is that to insure that 20-25% chance, you have to guess randomly. If you put 20 monkeys in a room to take this test, assuming they answered once per question and behaved themselves, on average they would get 20-25% of the questions correct. Put 20 test takers in the room, and the average will be much lower among guessed questions. Why?
1. The test writers intentionally write deceptive answer choices that "look" right. A test taker has no idea about a question, so picks the "best looking" answer, which is often wrong. The monkey has no idea what looks good and what doesn't, so will consistently be lucky about 20-25% of the time.
2. Test takers will eliminate answer choices from the guessing pool based on a hunch or intuition. Simple but correct answers often get excluded, leaving a 0% chance of being correct. The monkey has no clue, and often gets lucky with the best choice.

This is why the process of elimination endorsed by most test courses is flawed and detrimental to your performance- test takers don't guess, they make an ignorant stab in the dark that is usually worse than random.

$5 Challenge

Let me introduce one of the most valuable ideas of this course- the $5 challenge:

You only mark your "best guess" if you are willing to bet $5 on it.

You only eliminate choices from guessing if you are willing to bet $5 on it.

Why $5? Five dollars is an amount of money that is small yet not insignificant, and can really add up fast (20 questions could cost you $100). Likewise, each answer choice on one question of the test will have a small impact on your overall score, but it can really add up to a lot of points in the end.

The process of elimination IS valuable. The following shows your chance of guessing it right:

If you eliminate wrong answer choices until only this many remain:	Chance of getting it correct:
1	100%
2	50%
3	33%

However, if you accidentally eliminate the right answer or go on a hunch for an incorrect answer, your chances drop dramatically: to 0%. By guessing among all the answer choices, you are GUARANTEED to have a shot at the right answer.
That's why the $5 test is so valuable- if you give up the advantage and safety of a pure guess, it had better be worth the risk.

What we still haven't covered is how to be sure that whatever guess you make is truly random. Here's the easiest way:

Always pick the first answer choice among those remaining.
Such a technique means that you have decided, **before you see a single test question**, exactly how you are going to guess- and since the order of choices tells you nothing about which one is correct, this guessing technique is perfectly random.

This section is not meant to scare you away from making educated guesses or eliminating choices- you just need to define when a choice is worth eliminating. The $5 test, along with a pre-defined random guessing strategy, is the best way to make sure you reap all of the benefits of guessing.

Secret Key #3 - Practice Smarter, Not Harder

Many test takers delay the test preparation process because they dread the awful amounts of practice time they think necessary to succeed on the test. We have refined an effective method that will take you only a fraction of the time.

There are a number of "obstacles" in your way to succeed. Among these are answering questions, finishing in time, and mastering test-taking strategies. All must be executed on the day of the test at peak performance, or your score will suffer. The test is a mental marathon that has a large impact on your future.

Just like a marathon runner, it is important to work your way up to the full challenge. So first you just worry about questions, and then time, and finally strategy:

Success Strategy

1. Find a good source for practice tests.
2. If you are willing to make a larger time investment, consider using more than one study guide- often the different approaches of multiple authors will help you "get" difficult concepts.
3. Take a practice test with no time constraints, with all study helps "open book." Take your time with questions and focus on applying strategies.
4. Take a practice test with time constraints, with all guides "open book."
5. Take a final practice test with no open material and time limits

If you have time to take more practice tests, just repeat step 5. By gradually exposing yourself to the full rigors of the test environment, you will condition your mind to the stress of test day and maximize your success.

Secret Key #4 - Prepare, Don't Procrastinate

Let me state an obvious fact: if you take the test three times, you will get three different scores. This is due to the way you feel on test day, the level of preparedness you have, and, despite the test writers' claims to the contrary, some tests WILL be easier for you than others.

Since your future depends so much on your score, you should maximize your chances of success. In order to maximize the likelihood of success, you've got to prepare in advance. This means taking practice tests and spending time learning the information and test taking strategies you will need to succeed.

Never take the test as a "practice" test, expecting that you can just take it again if you need to. Feel free to take sample tests on your own, but when you go to take the official test, be prepared, be focused, and do your best the first time!

Secret Key #5 - Test Yourself

Everyone knows that time is money. There is no need to spend too much of your time or too little of your time preparing for the test. You should only spend as much of your precious time preparing as is necessary for you to get the score you need.

Once you have taken a practice test under real conditions of time constraints, then you will know if you are ready for the test or not.

If you have scored extremely high the first time that you take the practice test, then there is not much point in spending countless hours studying. You are already there.

Benchmark your abilities by retaking practice tests and seeing how much you have improved. Once you score high enough to guarantee success, then you are ready.

If you have scored well below where you need, then knuckle down and begin studying in earnest. Check your improvement regularly through the use of practice tests under real conditions. Above all, don't worry, panic, or give up. The key is perseverance!

Then, when you go to take the test, remain confident and remember how well you did on the practice tests. If you can score high enough on a practice test, then you can do the same on the real thing.

General Strategies

The most important thing you can do is to ignore your fears and jump into the test immediately- do not be overwhelmed by any strange-sounding terms. You have to jump into the test like jumping into a pool- all at once is the easiest way.

Make Predictions

As you read and understand the question, try to guess what the answer will be. Remember that several of the answer choices are wrong, and once you begin reading them, your mind will immediately become cluttered with answer choices designed to throw you off. Your mind is typically the most focused immediately after you have read the question and digested its contents. If you can, try to predict what the correct answer will be. You may be surprised at what you can predict.

Quickly scan the choices and see if your prediction is in the listed answer choices. If it is, then you can be quite confident that you have the right answer. It still won't hurt to check the other answer choices, but most of the time, you've got it!

Answer the Question

It may seem obvious to only pick answer choices that answer the question, but the test writers can create some excellent answer choices that are wrong. Don't pick an answer just because it sounds right, or you believe it to be true. It MUST answer the question. Once you've made your selection, always go back and check it against the question and make sure that you didn't misread the question, and the answer choice does answer the question posed.

Benchmark

After you read the first answer choice, decide if you think it sounds correct or not. If it doesn't, move on to the next answer choice. If it does, mentally mark that answer choice. This doesn't mean that you've definitely selected it as your answer choice, it just means that it's the best you've seen thus far. Go ahead and read the next choice. If the next choice is worse than the one you've already selected, keep going to the next answer choice. If the next choice is better than the choice you've already selected, mentally mark the new answer choice as your best guess.

The first answer choice that you select becomes your standard. Every other answer choice must be benchmarked against that standard. That choice is correct until proven otherwise by another answer choice beating it out. Once you've decided that no other answer choice seems as good, do one final check to ensure that your answer choice answers the question posed.

Valid Information

Don't discount any of the information provided in the question. Every piece of information may be necessary to determine the correct answer. None of the information in the question is there to throw you off (while the answer choices will certainly have information to throw you off). If two seemingly unrelated topics are discussed, don't ignore either. You can be confident there is a relationship, or it wouldn't be included in the question, and you are probably going to have to determine what is that relationship to find the answer.

Avoid "Fact Traps"

Don't get distracted by a choice that is factually true. Your search is for the answer that answers the question. Stay focused and don't fall for an answer that is true but incorrect. Always go back to the question and make sure you're choosing an answer that actually answers the question and is not just a true statement. An answer can be factually correct, but it MUST answer the question asked. Additionally, two answers can both be seemingly correct, so be sure to read all of the answer choices, and make sure that you get the one that BEST answers the question.

Milk the Question

Some of the questions may throw you completely off. They might deal with a subject you have not been exposed to, or one that you haven't reviewed in years. While your lack of knowledge about the subject will be a hindrance, the question itself can give you many clues that will help you find the correct answer. Read the question carefully and look for clues. Watch particularly for adjectives and nouns describing difficult terms or words that you don't recognize. Regardless of if you completely understand a word or not, replacing it with a synonym either provided or one you more familiar with may help you to understand what the questions are asking. Rather than wracking your mind about specific detailed information concerning a difficult term or word, try to use mental substitutes that are easier to understand.

The Trap of Familiarity

Don't just choose a word because you recognize it. On difficult questions, you may not recognize a number of words in the answer choices. The test writers don't put "make-believe" words on the test; so don't think that just because you only recognize all the words in one answer choice means that answer choice must be correct. If you only recognize words in one answer choice, then focus on that one. Is it correct? Try your best to determine if it is correct. If it is, that is great, but if it doesn't, eliminate it. Each word and answer choice you eliminate increases your chances of getting the question correct, even if you then have to guess among the unfamiliar choices.

Eliminate Answers

Eliminate choices as soon as you realize they are wrong. But be careful! Make sure you consider all of the possible answer choices. Just because one appears right, doesn't mean that the next one won't be even better! The test writers will usually put more than one good answer choice for every question, so read all of them. Don't worry if you are stuck between two that seem right. By getting down to just two remaining possible choices, your odds are now 50/50. Rather than wasting too much time, play the odds. You are guessing, but guessing wisely, because you've been able to knock out some of the answer choices that you know are wrong. If you are eliminating choices and realize that the last answer choice you are left with is also obviously wrong, don't panic. Start over and consider each choice again. There may easily be something that you missed the first time and will realize on the second pass.

Tough Questions

If you are stumped on a problem or it appears too hard or too difficult, don't waste time. Move on! Remember though, if you can quickly check for obviously incorrect answer choices, your chances of guessing correctly are greatly improved. Before you completely give up, at least try to knock out a couple of possible answers. Eliminate what you can and then guess at the remaining answer choices before moving on.

Brainstorm

If you get stuck on a difficult question, spend a few seconds quickly brainstorming. Run through the complete list of possible answer choices. Look at each choice and ask yourself, "Could this answer the question satisfactorily?" Go through each answer choice and consider it independently of the other. By systematically going through all possibilities, you may find something that you would otherwise overlook. Remember that when you get stuck, it's important to try to keep moving.

Read Carefully

Understand the problem. Read the question and answer choices carefully. Don't miss the question because you misread the terms. You have plenty of time to read each question thoroughly and make sure you understand what is being asked. Yet a happy medium must be attained, so don't waste too much time. You must read carefully, but efficiently.

Face Value

When in doubt, use common sense. Always accept the situation in the problem at face value. Don't read too much into it. These problems will not require you to make huge leaps of logic. The test writers aren't trying to throw you off with a cheap trick. If you have to go beyond creativity and make a leap of logic in order to have an answer choice answer the question, then you should look at the other answer choices. Don't overcomplicate the problem by creating theoretical relationships or explanations that will warp time or space. These are normal problems rooted in reality. It's just that the applicable relationship or explanation may not be readily apparent and you have to figure things out. Use your common sense to interpret anything that isn't clear.

Prefixes

If you're having trouble with a word in the question or answer choices, try dissecting it. Take advantage of every clue that the word might include. Prefixes and suffixes can be a huge help. Usually they allow you to determine a basic meaning. Pre- means before, post- means after, pro - is positive, de- is negative.

From these prefixes and suffixes, you can get an idea of the general meaning of the word and try to put it into context. Beware though of any traps. Just because con is the opposite of pro, doesn't necessarily mean congress is the opposite of progress!

Hedge Phrases

Watch out for critical "hedge" phrases, such as likely, may, can, will often, sometimes, often, almost, mostly, usually, generally, rarely, sometimes. Question writers insert these hedge phrases to cover every possibility. Often an answer choice will be wrong simply because it leaves no room for exception. Avoid answer choices that have definitive words like "exactly," and "always".

Switchback Words

Stay alert for "switchbacks". These are the words and phrases frequently used to alert you to shifts in thought. The most common switchback word is "but". Others include although, however, nevertheless, on the other hand, even though, while, in spite of, despite, regardless of.

New Information

Correct answer choices will rarely have completely new information included. Answer choices typically are straightforward reflections of the material asked about and will directly relate to the question. If a new piece of information is included in an answer choice that doesn't even seem to relate to the topic being asked about, then that answer choice is likely incorrect. All of the information needed to answer the question is usually provided for you, and so you should not have to make guesses that are unsupported or choose answer choices that require unknown information that cannot be reasoned on its own.

Time Management

On technical questions, don't get lost on the technical terms. Don't spend too much time on any one question. If you don't know what a term means, then since you don't have a dictionary, odds are you aren't going to get much further. You should immediately recognize terms as whether or not you know them. If you don't, work with the other clues that you have, the other answer choices and terms provided, but don't waste too much time trying to figure out a difficult term.

Contextual Clues

Look for contextual clues. An answer can be right but not correct. The contextual clues will help you find the answer that is most right and is correct. Understand the context in which a phrase or statement is made. This will help you make important distinctions.

Don't Panic

Panicking will not answer any questions for you. Therefore, it isn't helpful. When you first see the question, if your mind goes blank, take a deep breath. Force yourself to mechanically go through the steps of solving the problem and using the strategies you've learned.

Pace Yourself

Don't get clock fever. It's easy to be overwhelmed when you're looking at a page full of questions, your mind is full of random thoughts and feeling confused, and the clock is ticking down faster than you would like. Calm down and maintain the pace that you have set for yourself. As long as you are on track by monitoring your pace, you are guaranteed to have enough time for yourself. When you get to the last few minutes of the test, it may seem like you won't have enough time left, but if you only have as many questions as you should have left at that point, then you're right on track!

Answer Selection

The best way to pick an answer choice is to eliminate all of those that are wrong, until only one is left and confirm that is the correct answer. Sometimes though, an answer choice may immediately look right. Be careful! Take a second to make sure that the other choices are not equally obvious. Don't make a hasty mistake. There are only two times that you should stop before checking other answers. First is when you are positive that the answer choice you have selected is correct. Second is when time is almost out and you have to make a quick guess!

Check Your Work

Since you will probably not know every term listed and the answer to every question, it is important that you get credit for the ones that you do know. Don't miss any questions through careless mistakes. If at all possible, try to take a second to look back over your answer selection and make sure you've selected the correct answer choice and haven't made a costly careless mistake (such as marking an answer choice that you didn't mean to mark). This quick double check should more than pay for itself in caught mistakes for the time it costs.

Beware of Directly Quoted Answers

Sometimes an answer choice will repeat word for word a portion of the question or reference section. However, beware of such exact duplication – it may be a trap! More than likely, the correct choice will paraphrase or summarize a point, rather than being exactly the same wording.

Slang

Scientific sounding answers are better than slang ones. An answer choice that begins "To compare the outcomes…" is much more likely to be correct than one that begins "Because some people insisted…"

Extreme Statements

Avoid wild answers that throw out highly controversial ideas that are proclaimed as established fact. An answer choice that states the "process should be used in certain situations, if…" is much more likely to be correct than one that states the "process should be discontinued completely." The first is a calm rational statement and doesn't even make a definitive, uncompromising stance, using a hedge word "if" to provide wiggle room, whereas the second choice is a radical idea and far more extreme.

Answer Choice Families

When you have two or more answer choices that are direct opposites or parallels, one of them is usually the correct answer. For instance, if one answer choice states "x increases" and another answer choice states "x decreases" or "y increases," then those two or three answer choices are very similar in construction and fall into the same family of answer choices. A family of answer choices is when two or three answer choices are very similar in construction, and yet often have a directly opposite meaning. Usually the correct answer choice will be in that family of answer choices. The "odd man out" or answer choice that doesn't seem to fit the parallel construction of the other answer choices is more likely to be incorrect.

Special Report: How to Overcome Test Anxiety

The very nature of tests caters to some level of anxiety, nervousness or tension, just as we feel for any important event that occurs in our lives. A little bit of anxiety or nervousness can be a good thing. It helps us with motivation, and makes achievement just that much sweeter. However, too much anxiety can be a problem; especially if it hinders our ability to function and perform.

"Test anxiety," is the term that refers to the emotional reactions that some test-takers experience when faced with a test or exam. Having a fear of testing and exams is based upon a rational fear, since the test-taker's performance can shape the course of an academic career. Nevertheless, experiencing excessive fear of examinations will only interfere with the test-takers ability to perform, and his/her chances to be successful.

There are a large variety of causes that can contribute to the development and sensation of test anxiety. These include, but are not limited to lack of performance and worrying about issues surrounding the test.

Lack of Preparation

Lack of preparation can be identified by the following behaviors or situations:

- Not scheduling enough time to study, and therefore cramming the night before the test or exam
- Managing time poorly, to create the sensation that there is not enough time to do everything
- Failing to organize the text information in advance, so that the study material consists of the entire text and not simply the pertinent information
- Poor overall studying habits

Worrying, on the other hand, can be related to both the test taker, or many other factors around him/her that will be affected by the results of the test. These include worrying about:

- Previous performances on similar exams, or exams in general
- How friends and other students are achieving
- The negative consequences that will result from a poor grade or failure

There are three primary elements to test anxiety. Physical components, which involve the same typical bodily reactions as those to acute anxiety (to be discussed below). Emotional factors have to do with fear or panic. Mental or cognitive issues concerning attention spans and memory abilities.

Physical Signals

There are many different symptoms of test anxiety, and these are not limited to mental and emotional strain. Frequently there are a range of physical signals that will let a test taker know that he/she is suffering from test anxiety. These bodily changes can include the following:

- Perspiring
- Sweaty palms
- Wet, trembling hands
- Nausea
- Dry mouth
- A knot in the stomach
- Headache
- Faintness
- Muscle tension
- Aching shoulders, back and neck
- Rapid heart beat
- Feeling too hot/cold

To recognize the sensation of test anxiety, a test-taker should monitor him/herself for the following sensations:

- The physical distress symptoms as listed above
- Emotional sensitivity, expressing emotional feelings such as the need to cry or laugh too much, or a sensation of anger or helplessness
- A decreased ability to think, causing the test-taker to blank out or have racing thoughts that are hard to organize or control

Though most students will feel some level of anxiety when faced with a test or exam, the majority can cope with that anxiety and maintain it at a manageable level. However, those who cannot are faced with a very real and very serious condition, which can and should be controlled for the immeasurable benefit of this sufferer.

Naturally, these sensations lead to negative results for the testing experience. The most common effects of test anxiety have to do with nervousness and mental blocking.

Nervousness

Nervousness can appear in several different levels:

- The test-taker's difficulty, or even inability to read and understand the questions on the test
- The difficulty or inability to organize thoughts to a coherent form
- The difficulty or inability to recall key words and concepts relating to the testing questions (especially essays)
- The receipt of poor grades on a test, though the test material was well known by the test taker

Conversely, a person may also experience mental blocking, which involves:

- Blanking out on test questions
- Only remembering the correct answers to the questions when the test has already finished

Fortunately for test anxiety sufferers, beating these feelings, to a large degree, has to do with proper preparation. When a test taker has a feeling of preparedness, then anxiety will be dramatically lessened.

The first step to resolving anxiety issues is to distinguish which of the two types of anxiety are being suffered. If the anxiety is a direct result of a lack of preparation, this should be considered a normal reaction, and the anxiety level (as opposed to the test results) shouldn't be anything to worry about. However, if, when adequately prepared, the test-taker still panics, blanks out, or seems to overreact, this is not a fully rational reaction. While this can be considered normal too, there are many ways to combat and overcome these effects.

Remember that anxiety cannot be entirely eliminated, however, there are ways to minimize it, to make the anxiety easier to manage. Preparation is one of the best ways to minimize test anxiety. Therefore the following techniques are wise in order to best fight off any anxiety that may want to build.

To begin with, try to avoid cramming before a test, whenever it is possible. By trying to memorize an entire term's worth of information in one day, you'll be shocking your system, and not giving yourself a very good chance to absorb the information. This is an easy path to anxiety, so for those who suffer from test anxiety, cramming should not even be considered an option.

Instead of cramming, work throughout the semester to combine all of the material which is presented throughout the semester, and work on it gradually as the course goes by, making sure to master the main concepts first, leaving minor details for a week or so before the test.

To study for the upcoming exam, be sure to pose questions that may be on the examination, to gauge the ability to answer them by integrating the ideas from your texts, notes and lectures, as well as any supplementary readings.

If it is truly impossible to cover all of the information that was covered in that particular term, concentrate on the most important portions, that can be covered very well. Learn these concepts as best as possible, so that when the test comes, a goal can be made to use these concepts as presentations of your knowledge.

In addition to study habits, changes in attitude are critical to beating a struggle with test anxiety. In fact, an improvement of the perspective over the entire test-taking experience can actually help a test taker to enjoy studying and therefore improve the overall experience. Be certain not to overemphasize the significance of the grade - know that the result of the test is neither a reflection of self worth, nor is it a measure of intelligence; one grade will not predict a person's future success.

To improve an overall testing outlook, the following steps should be tried:

- Keeping in mind that the most reasonable expectation for taking a test is to expect to try to demonstrate as much of what you know as you possibly can.
- Reminding ourselves that a test is only one test; this is not the only one, and there will be others.
- The thought of thinking of oneself in an irrational, all-or-nothing term should be avoided at all costs.
- A reward should be designated for after the test, so there's something to look forward to. Whether it be going to a movie, going out to eat, or simply visiting friends, schedule it in advance, and do it no matter what result is expected on the exam

Test-takers should also keep in mind that the basics are some of the most important things, even beyond anti-anxiety techniques and studying. Never neglect the basic social, emotional and biological needs, in order to try to absorb information. In order to best achieve, these three factors must be held as just as important as the studying itself.

Study Steps

Remember the following important steps for studying:

- Maintain healthy nutrition and exercise habits. Continue both your recreational activities and social pass times. These both contribute to your physical and emotional well being.

- Be certain to get a good amount of sleep, especially the night before the test, because when you're overtired you are not able to perform to the best of your best ability.
- Keep the studying pace to a moderate level by taking breaks when they are needed, and varying the work whenever possible, to keep the mind fresh instead of getting bored.
- When enough studying has been done that all the material that can be learned has been learned, and the test taker is prepared for the test, stop studying and do something relaxing such as listening to music, watching a movie, or taking a warm bubble bath.

There are also many other techniques to minimize the uneasiness or apprehension that is experienced along with test anxiety before, during, or even after the examination. In fact, there are a great deal of things that can be done to stop anxiety from interfering with lifestyle and performance. Again, remember that anxiety will not be eliminated entirely, and it shouldn't be. Otherwise that "up" feeling for exams would not exist, and most of us depend on that sensation to perform better than usual. However, this anxiety has to be at a level that is manageable.

Of course, as we have just discussed, being prepared for the exam is half the battle right away. Attending all classes, finding out what knowledge will be expected on the exam, and knowing the exam schedules are easy steps to lowering anxiety. Keeping up with work will remove the need to cram, and efficient study habits will eliminate wasted time. Studying should be done in an ideal location for concentration, so that it is simple to become interested in the material and give it complete attention. A method such as SQ3R (Survey, Question, Read, Recite, Review) is a wonderful key to follow to make sure that the study habits are as effective as possible, especially in the case of learning from a textbook. Flashcards are great techniques for memorization. Learning to take good notes will mean that notes will be full of useful information, so that less sifting will need to be done to seek out what is pertinent for studying. Reviewing notes after class and then again on occasion will keep the information fresh in the mind. From notes that have been taken summary sheets and outlines can be made for simpler reviewing.

A study group can also be a very motivational and helpful place to study, as there will be a sharing of ideas, all of the minds can work together, to make sure that everyone understands, and the studying will be made more interesting because it will be a social occasion.

Basically, though, as long as the test-taker remains organized and self confident, with efficient study habits, less time will need to be spent studying, and higher grades will be achieved.

To become self confident, there are many useful steps. The first of these is "self talk." It has been shown through extensive research, that self-talk for students who suffer from test anxiety, should be well monitored, in order to make sure that it contributes to self confidence as opposed to sinking the student. Frequently the self talk of test-anxious students is negative or self-defeating, thinking that everyone else is smarter and faster, that they always mess up, and that if they don't do well, they'll fail the entire course. It is important to decreasing anxiety that awareness is made of self talk. Try writing any negative self thoughts and then disputing them with a positive statement instead. Begin self-encouragement as though it was a friend speaking. Repeat positive statements to help reprogram the mind to believing in successes instead of failures.

Helpful Techniques

Other extremely helpful techniques include:

- Self-visualization of doing well and reaching goals
- While aiming for an "A" level of understanding, don't try to "overprotect" by setting your expectations lower. This will only convince the mind to stop studying in order to meet the lower expectations.
- Don't make comparisons with the results or habits of other students. These are individual factors, and different things work for different people, causing different results.
- Strive to become an expert in learning what works well, and what can be done in order to improve. Consider collecting this data in a journal.
- Create rewards for after studying instead of doing things before studying that will only turn into avoidance behaviors.
- Make a practice of relaxing - by using methods such as progressive relaxation, self-hypnosis, guided imagery, etc - in order to make relaxation an automatic sensation.
- Work on creating a state of relaxed concentration so that concentrating will take on the focus of the mind, so that none will be wasted on worrying.
- Take good care of the physical self by eating well and getting enough sleep.
- Plan in time for exercise and stick to this plan.

Beyond these techniques, there are other methods to be used before, during and after the test that will help the test-taker perform well in addition to overcoming anxiety.

Before the exam comes the academic preparation. This involves establishing a study schedule and beginning at least one week before the actual date of the test.

By doing this, the anxiety of not having enough time to study for the test will be automatically eliminated. Moreover, this will make the studying a much more effective experience, ensuring that the learning will be an easier process. This relieves much undue pressure on the test-taker.

Summary sheets, note cards, and flash cards with the main concepts and examples of these main concepts should be prepared in advance of the actual studying time. A topic should never be eliminated from this process. By omitting a topic because it isn't expected to be on the test is only setting up the test-taker for anxiety should it actually appear on the exam. Utilize the course syllabus for laying out the topics that should be studied. Carefully go over the notes that were made in class, paying special attention to any of the issues that the professor took special care to emphasize while lecturing in class. In the textbooks, use the chapter review, or if possible, the chapter tests, to begin your review.

It may even be possible to ask the instructor what information will be covered on the exam, or what the format of the exam will be (for example, multiple choice, essay, free form, true-false). Additionally, see if it is possible to find out how many questions will be on the test. If a review sheet or sample test has been offered by the professor, make good use of it, above anything else, for the preparation for the test. Another great resource for getting to know the examination is reviewing tests from previous semesters. Use these tests to review, and aim to achieve a 100% score on each of the possible topics. With a few exceptions, the goal that you set for yourself is the highest one that you will reach.

Take all of the questions that were assigned as homework, and rework them to any other possible course material. The more problems reworked, the more skill and confidence will form as a result. When forming the solution to a problem, write out each of the steps. Don't simply do head work. By doing as many steps on paper as possible, much clarification and therefore confidence will be formed. Do this with as many homework problems as possible, before checking the answers. By checking the answer after each problem, a reinforcement will exist, that will not be on the exam. Study situations should be as exam-like as possible, to prime the test-taker's system for the experience. By waiting to check the answers at the end, a psychological advantage will be formed, to decrease the stress factor.

Another fantastic reason for not cramming is the avoidance of confusion in concepts, especially when it comes to mathematics. 8-10 hours of study will become one hundred percent more effective if it is spread out over a week or at least several days, instead of doing it all in one sitting. Recognize that the human brain requires time in order to assimilate new material, so frequent breaks and a span of study time over several days will be much more beneficial.

Additionally, don't study right up until the point of the exam. Studying should stop a minimum of one hour before the exam begins. This allows the brain to rest and put things in their proper order. This will also provide the time to become as relaxed as possible when going into the examination room. The test-taker will also have time to eat well and eat sensibly. Know that the brain needs food as much as the rest of the body. With enough food and enough sleep, as well as a relaxed attitude, the body and the mind are primed for success.

Avoid any anxious classmates who are talking about the exam. These students only spread anxiety, and are not worth sharing the anxious sentimentalities.

Before the test also involves creating a positive attitude, so mental preparation should also be a point of concentration. There are many keys to creating a positive attitude. Should fears become rushing in, make a visualization of taking the exam, doing well, and seeing an A written on the paper. Write out a list of affirmations that will bring a feeling of confidence, such as "I am doing well in my English class," "I studied well and know my material," "I enjoy this class." Even if the affirmations aren't believed at first, it sends a positive message to the subconscious which will result in an alteration of the overall belief system, which is the system that creates reality.

If a sensation of panic begins, work with the fear and imagine the very worst! Work through the entire scenario of not passing the test, failing the entire course, and dropping out of school, followed by not getting a job, and pushing a shopping cart through the dark alley where you'll live. This will place things into perspective! Then, practice deep breathing and create a visualization of the opposite situation - achieving an "A" on the exam, passing the entire course, receiving the degree at a graduation ceremony.

On the day of the test, there are many things to be done to ensure the best results, as well as the most calm outlook. The following stages are suggested in order to maximize test-taking potential:

- Begin the examination day with a moderate breakfast, and avoid any coffee or beverages with caffeine if the test taker is prone to jitters. Even people who are used to managing caffeine can feel jittery or light-headed when it is taken on a test day.
- Attempt to do something that is relaxing before the examination begins. As last minute cramming clouds the mastering of overall concepts, it is better to use this time to create a calming outlook.
- Be certain to arrive at the test location well in advance, in order to provide time to select a location that is away from doors, windows and other distractions, as well as giving enough time to relax before the test begins.

- Keep away from anxiety generating classmates who will upset the sensation of stability and relaxation that is being attempted before the exam.
- Should the waiting period before the exam begins cause anxiety, create a self-distraction by reading a light magazine or something else that is relaxing and simple.
- During the exam itself, read the entire exam from beginning to end, and find out how much time should be allotted to each individual problem. Once writing the exam, should more time be taken for a problem, it should be abandoned, in order to begin another problem. If there is time at the end, the unfinished problem can always be returned to and completed.

Read the instructions very carefully - twice - so that unpleasant surprises won't follow during or after the exam has ended.

When writing the exam, pretend that the situation is actually simply the completion of homework within a library, or at home. This will assist in forming a relaxed atmosphere, and will allow the brain extra focus for the complex thinking function.

Begin the exam with all of the questions with which the most confidence is felt. This will build the confidence level regarding the entire exam and will begin a quality momentum. This will also create encouragement for trying the problems where uncertainty resides.

Going with the "gut instinct" is always the way to go when solving a problem. Second guessing should be avoided at all costs. Have confidence in the ability to do well.

For essay questions, create an outline in advance that will keep the mind organized and make certain that all of the points are remembered. For multiple choice, read every answer, even if the correct one has been spotted - a better one may exist.

Continue at a pace that is reasonable and not rushed, in order to be able to work carefully. Provide enough time to go over the answers at the end, to check for small errors that can be corrected.

Should a feeling of panic begin, breathe deeply, and think of the feeling of the body releasing sand through its pores. Visualize a calm, peaceful place, and include all of the sights, sounds and sensations of this image. Continue the deep breathing, and take a few minutes to continue this with closed eyes. When all is well again, return to the test.

If a "blanking" occurs for a certain question, skip it and move on to the next question. There will be time to return to the other question later. Get everything done that can be done, first, to guarantee all the grades that can be compiled, and to build all of the confidence possible. Then return to the weaker questions to build the marks from there.

Remember, one's own reality can be created, so as long as the belief is there, success will follow. And remember: anxiety can happen later, right now, there's an exam to be written!

After the examination is complete, whether there is a feeling for a good grade or a bad grade, don't dwell on the exam, and be certain to follow through on the reward that was promised…and enjoy it! Don't dwell on any mistakes that have been made, as there is nothing that can be done at this point anyway.

Additionally, don't begin to study for the next test right away. Do something relaxing for a while, and let the mind relax and prepare itself to begin absorbing information again.
From the results of the exam - both the grade and the entire experience, be certain to learn from what has gone on. Perfect studying habits and work some more on confidence in order to make the next examination experience even better than the last one.

Learn to avoid places where openings occurred for laziness, procrastination and day dreaming.

Use the time between this exam and the next one to better learn to relax, even learning to relax on cue, so that any anxiety can be controlled during the next exam. Learn how to relax the body. Slouch in your chair if that helps. Tighten and then relax all of the different muscle groups, one group at a time, beginning with the feet and then working all the way up to the neck and face. This will ultimately relax the muscles more than they were to begin with. Learn how to breathe deeply and comfortably, and focus on this breathing going in and out as a relaxing thought. With every exhale, repeat the word "relax."

As common as test anxiety is, it is very possible to overcome it. Make yourself one of the test-takers who overcome this frustrating hindrance.

Additional Bonus Material

Due to our efforts to try to keep this book to a manageable length, we've created a link that will give you access to all of your additional bonus material.

Please visit http://www.mometrix.com/bonus948/priieleedipa to access the information.